THE ETERNAL FATHER AND HIS SON

BY

BRUCE E. DANA

THE ETERNAL FATHER AND HIS SON

BY

BRUCE E. DANA

CEDAR FORT

CFI
SPRINGVILLE, UTAH

Copyright © 2004 Bruce E. Dana

All Rights Reserved.

This book is not an official publication of
The Church of Jesus Christ of Latter-day Saints.

No part of this book may be reproduced in any form whatsoever, whether by graphic, visual, electronic, film, microfilm, tape recording, or any other means, without prior written permission of the author, except in the case of brief passages embodied in critical reviews and articles.

ISBN: 1-55517-788-3
e.1

Published by CFI
Imprint of Cedar Fort Inc.
www.cedarfort.com

Distributed by:

Cover design by Nicole Shaffer
Cover design © Lyle Mortimer
Edited by Janet M. Bernice

Printed in the United States of America
10 9 8 7 6 5 4 3 2 1

Printed on acid-free paper

Library of Congress number: 2004112351

Acknowledgements

As always, I am most indebted to my wife, Brenda, for allowing me valuable time to research and write. I am very appreciative for all of my family members—whose numbers happily keep increasing—for their constant love and support.

I am grateful to my publisher, Cedar Fort, Inc., for their confidence in publishing my previous five books. In particular, I am most appreciative to my dear friend, Dennis "C" Davis, who constantly shares his vast knowledge of the gospel with me, and reviews my writings so they will be doctrinally correct.

Table of Contents

1. Three Members Comprise the Godhead
   —The True Concept of God   1

2. Specific Roles Within the Godhead
   —Unity and Oneness in the Godhead   9

3. The Eternal Plan of Salvation
   —The Father Was Once a Mortal Man   17

4. Exalted Name—Titles of the Father
   —Man of Holiness   25

5. God the Father is a Heavenly Parent
   —Heavenly Father   35

6. Adam: A Son of God the Father
   —(Writings of Abraham and Moses)   43

7. Mary and God the Father
   —Mary and Eve   51

8. Conception of the Son of God
   —Born of a Virgin and the Eternal Father   57

9. The Father and His Mortal Son
   —Jesus Was Taught From on High   65

10. The Father Introduces His Beloved Son
    —A Grand Council in Heaven   73

11. Jesus Taught His Father's Doctrine
    —My Doctrine is Not Mine   85

12. Who Has Seen God the Father?
    —*Adam and Eve* — 93

13. Who Has Seen God's Son?
    —*Many Saw the Premortal Lord* — 101

14. Who Has Seen the Resurrected Lord?
    —*Mary Magdalene and Many Others* — 113

15. Who Has Seen the Lord in Our Day?
    —*(June 9, 1830 through Sept. 2, 1898)* — 125

16. Who Has Seen the Lord in Our Day?
    —*(October 3, 1918 through October 1, 1989)* — 137

17. God is Omnipotent
    —*Attribute of Power* — 147

18. The Fulness of the Father
    —*God's Son Did Not Receive a Fulness at First* — 155

Preface

Three personages comprise the Godhead or the Supreme Presidency of this universe: God the Father, God the Son, and God the Holy Ghost. Even though these three personages are gods, there is only one true and living God for us! He is our Heavenly Father.

One of the sacred and exalted name-titles of the first member of the Godhead is the Eternal Father. This special title combines in one expression the concept of God the Father as an eternal, exalted Man and his position as the literal Father of the spirits of all mankind. Because of his ability to produce spirit and physical bodies, this work will discuss how God is the literal Father of Adam and Eve and our Savior, Jesus Christ.

We are most thankful that our Father, as a mortal man, proved faithful to the eternal plan of salvation that was operational by His Heavenly Father; the same identical plan used by every God before him. We are especially thankful that the gospel of Jesus Christ allows each of us the same opportunity, based on our faithfulness, to become like our Heavenly Father.

This work will also discuss who has seen the Father and his Son, either in person or by vision. Therefore, let us begin our study of the Eternal Father and his Son.

Note

The author has frequently italicized words throughout this work for emphasis. Some of the teachings in this book are identical to those found in the author's other published books. The reason for this duplication is that it is the same gospel doctrine. In addition, the author previously obtained permission in his other books to quote several references. Therefore, in the endnote section of this work, the author has elected not to write permission obtained after each reference.

1

THREE MEMBERS COMPRISE THE GODHEAD—
THE TRUE CONCEPT OF GOD

In the Prophet Joseph Smith's time there were many different teachings concerning the Godhead. Let's consider a few of these.

Many people believed that the Father, Son, and Holy Ghost were one in the same person. Various preachers believed and taught that God no longer communicated with mankind. There were those who believed that God did not have a physical body, but was a spirit that was everywhere present. Besides these teachings, several taught that visions and revelations from God had ceased. In addition, there were individuals who did not even believe there was a God.

Regarding a prevalent teaching of that day, we turn to Elder Joseph Fielding Smith for information: "In the year 1820, when the First Vision was received [wherein the Father and the Son appeared to Joseph Smith, Jr.], the universal doctrine in the Protestant as well as the Catholic world, relating to the Godhead, in substance, was as follows:"

> There is *but one only living and true God* who is infinite in being and perfection, a most pure spirit, *invisible,*

THE ETERNAL FATHER AND HIS SON

without body, parts, or passions, immutable, *immense,* eternal, incomprehensible, almighty, most wise, most holy, most free, most absolute, working all things according to the counsel of his own immutable and most righteous will.[1]

To help us understand how these false God ideas developed, we need only to go back to the meridian of time, after our Lord was crucified. Both religious and secular history reveals how quickly priesthood leadership and authority was taken over by secular dominion. It also demonstrates how correct doctrines and ordinances were altered and distorted by human philosophies. Likewise, how quickly revelation from God to his apostles and prophets was replaced by uninspired councils of men penning creeds and teachings devoid of truth and reason.

Concerning the great apostasy, which had been prophesied, we use the words of Elder James E. Talmage:

The consistent, simple, and authentic doctrine respecting the character and attributes of God, such as was taught by Christ and the apostles, gave way as revelation ceased and as the darkness incident to the absence of divine authority fell upon the world, after the apostles and the Priesthood had been driven from the earth; and in its place appeared numerous theories and dogmas of men, many of which are utterly incomprehensible in their inconsistency and mysticism.

Giving specific examples, he says:

In the year 325, the Council of Nice was convened by the emperor Constantine, who sought through this body to secure a declaration of Christian belief that would be received as authoritative, and be the means of arresting the increasing dissension incident to the *prevalent disagreement regarding the nature of the Godhead* and other theological subjects. The Council condemned some of the theories then current, including that of Arius, which asserted that the Son was created by the Father, and therefore could not be coeternal with the Father. The Council promulgated what is known as the Nicene Creed; and this was followed in time by the Athanasian Creed over which, however, controversy has arisen as to authorship. The creed follows: 'We worship one God in Trinity, and Trinity in Unity, neither confounding the persons, nor dividing the substance. For there is one person of the Father, another of the Son, and another of the Holy Ghost. But the Godhead of the Father, Son, and Holy Ghost, is all one; the glory equal, the majesty co-eternal. Such as the Father is, such is the Son, and such is the Holy Ghost. The Father uncreate, the Son uncreate, and the Holy Ghost uncreate. The Father incomprehensible, the Son incomprehensible, and the Holy Ghost incomprehensible. The Father eternal, the Son eternal, and the Holy Ghost eternal. And yet there are not three eternals, but one eternal. As also there are not three incomprehensibles, nor three uncreated; but one uncreated, and one incomprehensible. So likewise the Father is Almighty, the Son Almighty, and the Holy Ghost Almighty; and yet they are not three Almighties, but one Almighty. So the Father is God, the Son is God, and the Holy Ghost is God, and yet there are not three Gods but one God.

Elder Talmage then gives his personal thoughts on the matter: "It would be difficult to conceive of a greater number of inconsistencies and contradictions expressed in words as few."

He strongly declares: "We affirm that to deny the materiality of God's person is to deny God; for a thing without parts has no whole and an immaterial body cannot exist."[2]

Several centuries following these different creeds, various individuals began to question and disagree with this type of false

THE ETERNAL FATHER AND HIS SON

thinking. Concerning the Reformation movement, Elder Milton R. Hunter said:

> ... the glorious Gospel truths proclaimed by the Savior were corrupted by pagan teachings and practices to such an extent that Isaiah's prophecy was completely fulfilled wherein he declared: *'The earth also is defiled under the inhabitants thereof; because they have transgressed the laws, changed the ordinance, broken the everlasting covenant'* (Isaiah 24: 5).
>
> These facts became apparent to a number of good men, such as Martin Luther, John Calvin, William Tyndale, the Wesley brothers, and others, who inaugurated what is known as the Reformation. Through sincere and diligent efforts they attempted to restore the Gospel teachings and practices to what the Master had given. But none of them held the holy Priesthood of God, which was absolutely essential if they were officially to establish the true Church of Jesus Christ ... As time passed the Christian teachers violently disagreed with each other on many points of doctrine, with the result that numerous Christian denominations came into existence. What was badly needed—in fact, positively essential—was the restoration of the Priesthood from heaven and a new revelation of God's will.[3]

In conjunction with Elder Hunter's words, Joseph Smith, Jr. explains what happened when he was age fourteen. He says that in the second year after his family moved to Manchester, New York, there was in that place an unusual excitement on the subject of religion. Great multitudes of people were contending for the Methodist faith, and some for the Presbyterian, and some for the Baptist.

Seriously pondering about the total religious confusion of his time, young Joseph asked: "If any one of [these religious sects] be right, which is it, and how shall I know it?" In a grove of trees near his family home, this young lad knelt in prayer seeking information. A glorious vision came as an answer, wherein the boy-prophet solemnly declares:

"*I saw two Personages* . . . *standing above me in the air.*" Once again the divine testimony of the Father was heard: "*This is My Beloved Son. Hear Him!*" ("Joseph Smith—History" 1: 10-17)

PHYSICAL ATTRIBUTES OF THE FATHER AND SON

Once again the true concept of God was revealed anew in this the final dispensation of times. To help describe the physical attributes of the Father—which equally applies to the Son—President George Q. Cannon, First Counselor to President John Taylor, said:

"Joseph saw that the Father had a form; that He had a head; that He had arms; that He had limbs; that He had feet; that He had a face and a tongue with which to express His thoughts; for He said unto Joseph: 'This is my beloved Son'—pointing to the Son—'hear Him.'" [4]

Previous to this description, President Brigham Young stated: "We differ from them [other religions] in our ideas of God. We know that he is a Being—a man—with all the component parts of an intelligent being—head, hair, eyes, ears, nose, mouth, cheek bones, forehead, chin, body, lower limbs; that he eats, drinks, talks, lives and has a being, and has a residence . . ." [5]

As previously written, the Prophet declared: "*I saw two Personages . . . standing above me in the air.*" With this knowledge, we discover that gravity, as we know it, does not have the same force and influence on resurrected beings as it does mortals. To help better understand the ability of the Father and the Son to stand in the air, Elder Orson Pratt wrote:

> Man has legs, so has God . . . Man walks with his legs, so does God sometimes . . . God can not only walk, *but he can move up and down through the air without using his legs as in the* process of walking . . . God, though in the figure of a man, has many powers that man has not got. He can *go upwards through the air.* He can *waft* [move] himself from world to world by his own self-moving powers. These are powers not possessed by man only through faith, as in the instances of Enoch and Elijah. Therefore, though in the figure of a man, *he has powers far superior to man.*[6]

Therefore, the Prophet Joseph Smith was able to see that the Father and Son were separate, glorified men, who have physical bodies identical in form to mortal man. In addition, these two Personages were able to move and verbally communicate to him in his own language.

Once again, revelation answered the boy-prophet's question: "Which of all the [different churches] was right . . . and which I should join." The Lord verbally told Joseph: "I must join none of them, *for they were all wrong*" ("Joseph Smith—History" 1: 18-19).

Following this glorious appearance of the Father and the Son, the boy-prophet explains what transpired: "Some few days after I had this vision, I happened to be in company with one of the Methodist preachers . . . and, conversing with him on the subject of religion, I took occasion to give him an account of the vision which I had had."

Regarding this preacher's reaction, Joseph explains: "I was greatly surprised at his behavior; he treated my communications not only lightly, but with great contempt, saying it was all of the devil, *that there were no such things as visions or revelations in these days;* that all such things had ceased with the apostles, *and that there would never be any more of them*" ("Joseph Smith—History" 1:5-21).

In stark contrast from what this preacher said, that revelations and visions had ceased, the Prophet solemnly declares, "For I had seen a vision; I knew it, and I knew that God knew it, and I could not deny it . . ." ("Joseph Smith—History" 1: 25)

Concerning this glorious vision, we use the words of President Heber J. Grant: "The vision was a reality and direct. When Joseph received it, men were loath [reluctant] to believe that it was possible for God or holy beings to speak to man on the earth . . ."[7]

It is important for us to understand that this vision was not even a vision in the sense we normally speak of visions. The Father and his Son appeared to the Prophet Joseph Smith literally and physically. Therefore, in the spring of 1820, as Elder Joseph Fielding Smith appropriately wrote:

> . . . after the vision was given to Joseph Smith of the Father and the Son, *he stood the only witness among men who could testify with knowledge that God lives and Jesus Christ is verily his Son. In this knowledge he became a special witness for Christ, and thus an apostle before the Priesthood had been restored* . . . .[8]

Therefore, from the comments spoken by the preacher to the boy-prophet, along with the previously cited religious creeds, we have a better understanding of the false teachings that were expressed in the year 1820 concerning the Godhead. To reiterate, the true concept of God was revealed anew to the Prophet Joseph Smith, for he personally saw the Father and his

THE ETERNAL FATHER AND HIS SON

Son in the Sacred Grove. As such, he solemnly testified that they are separate, glorified men, who have bodies identical in form to mortal man. In addition, he says that they were able to move and verbally communicated with him in his own language, and they gave him specific instructions and teachings. Therefore, as Elder Joseph Fielding Smith has appropriately written, Joseph was the only witness who could testify with knowledge that God lives and Jesus Christ is verily his Son.

2

SPECIFIC ROLES WITHIN THE GODHEAD—
UNITY AND ONENESS IN THE GODHEAD

At the request of Mr. John Wentworth, Editor and Proprietor of a newspaper, *Chicago Democrat*, the Prophet Joseph Smith wrote a short but remarkably full history of the leading events in the Church, along with thirteen brief statements which summarize some of the basic doctrines of The Church of Jesus Christ of Latter-day Saints. The Wentworth letter was first published in the *Times and Seasons* of March 1, 1842 and is classified as one of the most inspired documents ever written by the Prophet. [9]

These thirteen brief statements are called the Articles of Faith. Regarding the First Article of Faith, President Gordon B. Hinckley, who was then First Counselor to President Ezra Taft Benson, wrote:

"It is the pivotal position of our religion. It is significant that in setting forth the primary elements of our doctrine, the Prophet Joseph put this as number one. '*We believe in God, the*

THE ETERNAL FATHER AND HIS SON

Eternal Father, and in His Son, Jesus Christ, and in the Holy Ghost."[10]

From doctrines taught by the Prophet, members of the Church know that three, separate personages comprise the Godhead—The Father, Son, and Holy Ghost. However, there are some who are confused by the scripture found in the Book of Mormon which reads: "And now, behold, this is the doctrine of Christ, and the only and true doctrine of the Father, and of the Son, and of the Holy Ghost, *which is one God*" (2 Nephi 31: 21, italics added). Likewise, our Lord declared to the Jews: "*I and my Father are one*" (John 10: 30).

In addition, the three witnesses to the Book of Mormon have written in their combined testimony: "And the honor be to the Father, and to the Son, and to the Holy Ghost, *which is one God.*"

To help clarify these statements, we turn to President Charles W. Penrose, First Counselor to President Heber J. Grant, for understanding:

> *There is the oneness of Deity*, the three in one; not as some preachers try to expound it, in the doctrines of the outside world, in the Article of Faith that they have, making them one immaterial spirit—no body, no real personage, no substance. On the contrary, *they are three individuals*, one in spirit, one in mind, one in intelligence, *united in all things that they do*, and it takes the Father, the Son, and the Holy Ghost, to make the perfect Trinity in one, three persons and one God or Deity, *one Godhead.*[11]

Even in our day, various religions teach the doctrine of the Trinity. However, their belief is that they are one in the same person, who performs three functions, according to his holy will.

Continuing our study of the oneness of the Godhead, we read the words of Elder Bruce R. McConkie:

> Three glorious persons comprise the Godhead or supreme presidency of the universe. They are the Father, the Son, and the Holy Ghost. Each one possesses the same divine nature, knows all things, and has all power. Each one has the same character, the same perfections, and the same attributes. In Christ, Paul says: 'dwelleth all the fulness of the Godhead bodily' (Colossians 2:9). *Because of this perfect unity, they are spoken of as being one God* . . . Thus Jesus prayed for all true believers, 'that they all may be one; as thou, Father, art in me, and I in thee, that they also may be one in us' (John 17: 21).[12]

In speaking of unity, the Lord tells the Latter-day Saints: "I say unto you, be one; and if ye are not one ye are not mine" (D&C 38: 27). From these teachings, we are properly taught the perfect unity of the Godhead; and at times, we are also taught why they are spoken of as being one God.

We now turn our attention to the gospel of Matthew, wherein we are properly taught that the members of the Godhead are separate individuals. This apostolic writer informs us that Jesus came from Galilee to a river named Jordan to be baptized of John. Knowing that Jesus was the Messiah, John said to our Lord, "I have need to be baptized of thee, and comest thou to me?"

Jesus answered him: "Suffer it to be so now: for thus it becometh us to fulfil all righteousness."

Accordingly, both John and Jesus entered into the river Jordan, and Jesus was totally immersed in the water by John. After our Lord was baptized, he straightway came out of the water and the heavens were opened and the Spirit of God was seen descending like a dove.

Then, a voice from heaven was heard saying, *"This is my beloved Son, in whom I am well pleased"* (Matthew 3: 13-17).

Regarding this special scene, Elder McConkie wrote: "Our Lord's baptism is one of the classical illustrations of the separate

THE ETERNAL FATHER AND HIS SON

and distinct individualities who comprise the eternal Godhead. Jesus is present in mortality; the personage of the Holy Ghost is seen descending from heaven to be with him; and the voice of the Father is heard introducing his Son to the world."[13]

From the Prophet Joseph Smith, we are informed of specific roles within the Godhead. An everlasting covenant was made between three personages before the organization of this earth, and it relates to their dispensation of things to men on this particular earth; "these personages, according the Abraham's record, are called *God the first, the Creator;* God the second, the Redeemer; and God the third, the witness or Testator."[14]

Though the Father delegated to the Son and other spirits to perform many of the creative acts on our earth, it does not make these other creators independent of the Father as the Creator of all things.[15]

To demonstrate this, we turn to the writings of Moses, as recorded in the *Pearl of Great Price*, wherein "he saw God face to face, and he talked with him, and the glory of God was upon Moses; therefore Moses could endure his presence" (Moses 1: 2). During this glorious visit, "Moses cast his eyes and beheld the earth, yea, even all of it . . . discerning it by the spirit of God. And he beheld also the inhabitants thereof, and there was not a soul which he beheld not . . . and he discerned them by the spirit of God" (Moses 1: 27-28).

Seeking knowledge, this mighty prophet asked: "Tell me, I pray thee, why these things are so, and by what thou madest them?"

The Lord God responded: "For mine own purpose have I made these things . . . And by the word of my power, have I created them, which is mine Only Begotten Son, who is full of grace and truth.

"And worlds without number have I created . . . and by the Son I created them . . . But only an account of this earth, and the inhabitants thereof, give I unto you . . ." (Moses 1: 30-35).

Concerning these scriptures, some have wondered if Moses was speaking to God the Father or Jehovah. The answer is provided by Elder Joseph Fielding Smith:

> All revelation since the fall [of Adam] has come through Jesus Christ, who is the Jehovah of the Old Testament. In all of the scriptures, where God is mentioned and where he has appeared, it was Jehovah who talked with Abraham, with Noah, Enoch, Moses and all the prophets . . . *The Father has never dealt with man directly and personally since the fall, and he has never appeared except to introduce and bear record of the Son.* Thus the *Inspired Version* of the *Bible* [which is now called the *Joseph Smith Translation*] records that 'no man hath seen God at any time, except he hath borne record of the Son . . .'[16] (JST John 1:19).

Therefore, by divine investiture of authority, Jehovah spoke to this mighty prophet as though he were the Father.[17] From this writing of Moses, we discover that the Father is the Creator of this earth, but he delegated the creative process to the Son.

We are further informed from Elder McConkie that there are two creative events that are exclusively the Father's:

> First, he is the Father of all spirits, Christ's included; none were fathered or created by anyone else. Second, he is the Creator of the physical body of man. Though Jehovah and Michael and many of the noble and great ones played their assigned roles in the various creative events, yet when it came time to place man on earth, the Lord God [who is the Father] himself performed the creative acts. 'I, God, created man in mine own image, in the image of mine Only Begotten created I him; male and female created I them' (Moses 2:27).[18]

THE ETERNAL FATHER AND HIS SON

Continuing, Elder McConkie says,

> Only the Father is or could be the author of the plan of salvation. He alone was in a position to ordain the laws and establish the system whereby his spirit children (Christ included!) could be saved.[19]

TO KNOW THE ONLY TRUE GOD

With this understanding, we turn our attention to one of the greatest prayers ever recorded in mortality, the *Intercessory Prayer*, wherein Jesus said: "And this is life eternal, *that they might know thee the only true God*, and Jesus Christ, whom thou hast sent" (John 17: 3).

The true order of prayer is that we pray to the Father, in the name of his Son, by the power of the Holy Ghost. Here, Jesus is following this true order—he is praying to his Father, in his own name, and every word is spoken by the power of the Holy Ghost. Accordingly, each member of the Godhead performs an important function and service for mankind when men and women follow the true order of prayer.

To help clarify our Savior's statement, *"that they might know thee the only true God,"* we again turn to the expressions of Elder McConkie:

> In the ultimate and final sense of the word, there is only one true and living God. He is the Father, the Almighty Elohim, the Supreme Being, the Creator and Ruler of the universe. Paul said: ' There is none other God but one. For though there be [others] that are called gods, whether in heaven or in earth (as there be gods many, and lords many,) but to us there is but one God, the Father, of whom are all things, and we in him; and one Lord Jesus Christ, by whom are all things, and we by

him. Howbeit there is not in every man that knowledge' (1 Corinthians 8:4-7).

Continuing his explanation, we read:

Christ is God; he alone is the Savior. The Holy Ghost is God; he is one with the Father and the Son. But these two are the second and third members of the Godhead. *The Father is God above all, and is, in fact, the God of the Son.* Indeed, the resurrected Christ said to Mary Magdalene: 'I ascend unto my Father, and your Father; and to my God, and your God' (John 20:17). And also: 'I go unto the Father: for my Father is greater than I' (John 14:28). And yet again: 'My Father . . . is greater than all' (John 10:29). Our apostolic scholar then writes that Paul is saying that the Father is the one God who is supreme; that he is the God of Jesus Christ, who also is a God.[20]

Concerning the physical attributes of the members of the Godhead, the Prophet says: "The Father has a body of flesh and bones as tangible as man's; the Son also; but the Holy Ghost has not a body of flesh and bones, but is a personage of Spirit. Were it not so, the Holy Ghost could not dwell in us" (D&C 130:22).

From this descriptive doctrine, we know that when the Prophet Joseph Smith saw the Father and Son in the Sacred Grove, they were glorified, resurrected men, who had bodies of flesh and bones ("Joseph Smith—History" 1:17). In addition, from the above mentioned scripture, we are informed that the Holy Ghost is a personage of Spirit—a spirit man. As such, he testifies of the Father and Son by the means of his Spirit speaking to the spirit housed in our mortal body.

Specifically speaking of the third member of the Godhead, Elder B. H. Roberts has written this description:

... the Holy Ghost, not a tabernacle of flesh and bone, but doubtless of form and features as the [Father and Son], but spirit throughout. So in the [Godhead] there is one personage who has a special office, who exercises a special function that enables him to come close to your spirit and my spirit. He penetrates all external things and unites with our spirits, and so vibrates in our spiritual life, that he testifies of the truth, testifies of the Father; testifies for the whole truth of the gospel scheme; testifies of the being and nature of the Father and of the Son. *He is a witness to the souls of men of all these truths.* In the witness which the Holy Ghost bears it is as if the very soul of God was united with the soul of man, bearing witness of the truth; and doubtless in the exercise of this witnessing function the Holy Ghost is more powerful than any other agency whatsoever in making known the truth. And that is why a sin against the Holy Ghost is so awful in its consequences.[21]

From teachings given by the Prophet Joseph Smith, along with various scriptures written, we know that three, separate individuals comprise the Godhead—The Father, Son, and Holy Ghost. According to Abraham's record, they are known as *God the first, the Creator*; God the second, the Redeemer; and God the third, the witness or Testator. Accordingly, we are informed of specific roles within the Godhead. As such, we know that God the Father is the supreme member of the Godhead, for he is the Creator.

3

THE ETERNAL PLAN OF SALVATION—
THE FATHER WAS ONCE A MORTAL MAN

As to the Father's glorified status as an exalted man, as to how he attained his position of supreme prominence, and as to how each of us can pursue the same eternal course and obtain the same exalted destiny, we turn to the Prophet Joseph Smith for knowledge. At the April 7, 1844 Conference of the Church held in Nauvoo, Illinois, the Prophet preached one of the greatest sermons ever recorded. Speaking before nearly 20,000 members, he revealed the nature and kind of being that God is and told how man, as a joint-heir with our Lord, may become like the Father.[22]

It is important to understand that the teachings spoken by the Prophet at this General Conference were new to a majority of the members of the Church. The Church of Jesus Christ of Latter-day Saints was still in its infancy, having been formally organized fourteen years earlier on April 6, 1830, at Fayette, New York.[23] Concerning Nauvoo in 1844, Elder Joseph Fielding Smith says: "Through the gathering of converts from Great

THE ETERNAL FATHER AND HIS SON

Britain as well as from various parts of the United States, Nauvoo had become the foremost city of Illinois. It had risen from a swamp and wilderness in 1839, to a commonwealth of some twenty thousand souls."[24]

Therefore, the Prophet Joseph Smith was speaking at this Conference to nearly every convert member of the Church who heeded the call to come to Nauvoo.

After giving preliminary remarks, the Prophet said: "It is necessary for us to have an understanding of God himself in the beginning. If we start right, it is easy to go right all the time . . .

"If men do not comprehend the character of God, they do not comprehend themselves. I want to go back to the beginning, and so lift your minds into a more lofty sphere and a more exalted understanding than what the human mind generally aspires to."

Later in his discourse he reiterates: "I will go back to the beginning before the world was, to show what kind of being God is . . . "

> *God himself was once as we are now, and is an exalted man, and sits enthroned in yonder heavens! That is the great secret. If the veil was rent today, and the great God who holds this world in its orbit, and who upholds all worlds and all things by his power, was to make himself visible,—I say, if you were to see him today, you would see him like a man in form—like yourselves in all the person, image, and very form as a man; for Adam was created in the very fashion, image and likeness of God, and received instructions from, and walked, talked and conversed with him, as one man talks and communes with another . . .*[25]

We may safely believe that most of the members in this congregation had heard the First Vision account, wherein Joseph personally saw the Father and his Son in the Sacred Grove.[26] However, we may also safely believe that the majority of the

Saints had never heard that God was once as they were. This was a new and marvelous doctrine to these faithful members of the Church. Knowing this, the Prophet stated:

> *These are incomprehensible ideas to some*, but they are simple. It is the first principle of the Gospel to know for a certainty the Character of God, and to know that we may converse with him as one man converses with another, and that *he was once a man like us; yea, that God himself, the Father of us all, dwelt on an earth, the same as Jesus Christ himself did; and I will show it from the Bible.*[27]

Again, we may safely believe that the majority of these early Saints did not know that God the Father once lived on an earth as a mortal being, the same as Jesus did. These truly were marvelous teachings being revealed by the Lord's chosen servant.

THE DIVINE PATRIARCHAL ORDER OF ETERNITY

By reason that our Father in Heaven once lived on an earth as a mortal man, he experienced challenges and trials like we are going through in our mortality. To support this thinking, we use the words of President Joseph F. Smith: "We are the children of God. He is an eternal being . . . *We are precisely in the same condition and under the same circumstances that God our Heavenly Father was when he was passing through this or a similar ordeal.*"[28] (Italics added).

Giving additional insight on this subject, President Brigham Young revealed the following doctrine:

> The great architect, manager and superintendent . . . who guides this work is out of sight to our natural eyes. He lives on another world; he is in another state of

existence; *he has passed the ordeals we are now passing through; he has received an experience, has suffered and enjoyed, and knows all that we know regarding the toils, sufferings, life and death of this mortality, for he has passed through the whole of it, and has received his crown and exaltation . . .*[29]

Because our Heavenly Father earned his exaltation and was crowned a God, he implemented the same eternal plan of salvation that will allow his offspring the same opportunity to become like him. For as the Prophet Joseph Smith has explained: "God himself, finding he was in the midst of spirits [which is our Father's spirit children] . . . *saw proper to institute laws whereby the rest could have a privilege to advance like himself.* The relationship we have with God places us in a situation to advance in knowledge [the same as our Father has advanced in knowledge]. He has power to institute laws to instruct . . .[his spirit children who have not yet obtained exaltation] *that they may be exalted with himself,* so that they might have one glory upon another, and all that knowledge, power, glory, and intelligence, which is requisite in order to save them . . ."[30]

When this glorious plan of salvation was presented by the Father to his spirit children, we are informed by President Joseph F. Smith, that "there was nothing in it . . . that was superfluous or unnecessary; nothing in it that could be dispensed with; *it was a complete plan devised . . . for the redemption of the human race and for their salvation and exaltation in the presence of God.*"[31]

It is important for each of us to know that this same eternal plan allowed our Father, as a mortal man, to become our Heavenly Father. To support this belief, we use the inspired words of President George Q. Cannon, First Counselor to President John Taylor: "We must remember that God's work is not confined to this life; *that God's plan of salvation extends throughout eternity; that according to our belief it began to operate in eternity . . . it always operated, operated from eternity and will operate to eternity . . ."*[32]

Giving further evidence that it is an eternal plan of salvation, Hyrum Andrus, a recognized LDS scholar, expressed the following thoughts concerning the divine patriarchal order of eternity:

When exalted man attains the power of eternal lives—the continuation of posterity forever and ever—in the resurrection, he will have power within the realm of spirits to organize, through procreation, spirit children over whom he will preside as a father and a god (D&C 132). *His spirit children will then have the same relationship to him that man had to Elohim* [who is our Heavenly Father] *in the pre-earth existence.*

Brother Andrus then expresses these thoughts concerning this glorious plan: "Those who attain an exaltation in the celestial kingdom will also have the responsibility of guiding and directing their spirit children through the further experiences of life that are necessary in acquiring physical bodies and rising to exaltation in the midst of celestial glory.

"Herein is portrayed the eternal cycle of organized life that has been continuing from all eternity, and that will continue to all eternity. There is therefore *a patriarchal line of deities,* one generation above another, without end . . ."[33]

In support of this doctrine, the Prophet Joseph Smith said: "If [the Old Testament prophet] Abraham reasoned thus—*If Jesus Christ was the Son of God, and John* [the Revelator] *discovered that God the Father of Jesus Christ had a Father, you may suppose that he had a Father also. . . ."*[34]

As we notice, the first letter of the word Father is capitalized. Though it is true that our Father in Heaven once had an earthly father, the word Father, as used by the Prophet, means Heavenly Father. To support this statement, we again use the Prophet's

THE ETERNAL FATHER AND HIS SON

words: "Paul [the New Testament apostle] *says that which is earthly is in the likeness of that which is heavenly.* Hence if Jesus had a Father [which is also our Heavenly Father], can we not believe that *He* [our Heavenly Father] had a [Heavenly] Father also? I despise the idea of being scared to death at such a doctrine, for the Bible is full of it."[35]

Revealing fascinating doctrine, the Prophet further declared: "I want you to pay particular attention to what I am saying. Jesus said that the Father [who is our Heavenly Father] wrought precisely in the same way as His [Heavenly] Father had done before him." Posing it as a question, the Prophet asked, "As the Father had done before?" Answering his own question, he says, "He [our Heavenly Father] laid down His life, and took it up the same as His [Heavenly] Father had done before. He [our Heavenly Father] did as He was sent, to lay down his life and take it up again; and then was committed unto Him [our Heavenly Father] the keys [authority that all Gods receive in order to be a Heavenly Father]."[36]

In addition to these profound teachings given by the Prophet Joseph, President Brigham Young declared: "How many Gods there are, I do not know. But there never was a time when there were not Gods and worlds, and when men were not passing through the same ordeals that we are now passing through. *That course has been from eternity, and it is and will be to all eternity.* You cannot comprehend this, but when you can, it will be to you a matter of great consolation."[37]

In another sermon, President Young provided further insight on this glorious subject: "It is written, 'Prove all things, hold fast that which is good.' Refuse evil, choose good, hate iniquity, love truth. All this our fathers have done before us; I do not particularly mean Father Adam, or his Father [which is our Heavenly Father] [38]; I do not particularly mean Abraham, or Moses, the Prophets, or Apostles, *but I mean our fathers who have been exalted for millions of years previous to Adam's time*. They have all passed through the same ordeals we are now passing through . . . ."[39]

The plan of salvation, for mankind in this life, is the gospel of Jesus Christ. It comprises all of the laws, ordinances, and performances that are necessary for our Father's children to gain eternal life and become like him.

Concerning this belief, then bishop Orson F. Whitney expressed these inspiring teachings: "The exclusiveness which the Latter-day Saints exhibits is this: they maintain that the Lord has but one way to save the human race; that the term 'everlasting gospel' is not a misnomer, but means exactly what it says, *and that it is eternal as its maker or framer is eternal. It can no more change than He can change. A man* [or woman] *must obey the same principles now that were obeyed two thousand years ago, or six thousand years ago, or millions of ages ago, in order to attain the presence of His* [Jesus Christ's] *Father and God* [who is our Heavenly Father]. *There is but one way, one plan of life and salvation, and there need be but one*; for God, being an economist, does not create that which is superfluous; and there can be, in the very nature of things, only one true plan of eternal life." Bishop Whitney then adds this significant statement: "Of a necessity God [our Heavenly Father] is the author of perfection; His works are not deficient in any respect, and what He ordains for the salvation of [mankind] is the only way for [mankind] to be saved. *Thus it is that the Latter-day Saints preach the everlasting gospel, the unchangeable way of eternal life* . . . ."[40]

From all of these inspired teachings, we are correctly taught that the Father's plan of salvation is an eternal plan; the same identical plan that allowed our Father to gain exaltation and become our Heavenly Father. By reason that he is our Heavenly Father, his work and glory is "to bring to pass the immortality and eternal life of man" (Moses 1:39). As Brother Hyrum

THE ETERNAL FATHER AND HIS SON

Andrus says: "Those who attain an exaltation in the celestial kingdom will also have the responsibility of guiding and directing their spirit offspring through further experiences of life that are necessary in acquiring physical bodies and rising to exaltation in the midst of celestial glory." [41]

Thus, the divine patriarchal order of eternity, for those who become a God, is clearly set forth. We are most thankful that our Father, as a mortal man, proved faithful to the eternal plan of salvation that was operational by his Heavenly Father; the same identical plan used by all the Fathers before him. We are especially thankful that this eternal plan of salvation allows each of us the same opportunity, based on our faithfulness, to become like our Heavenly Father!

4

EXALTED NAME—
TITLES OF THE FATHER—
MAN OF HOLINESS

In all respects, the Son of God is like his Father. They both look alike; each is in the express image of each other. They think alike; they speak the same eternal truths; and every action taken by the one is the same thing the other would do under the same circumstances (John 12:44-45; 14:6-20). By divine investiture of authority, our Lord has spoken at times as though he was the Father. Though the Father and Son think and act with complete oneness, we noticed that during his mortal ministry, Jesus identified himself, at least seventy times, as the Son of Man. To justify himself and his disciples in violating the strict Jewish rules concerning Sabbath observances, our Lord said: "Therefore the Son of man is Lord also of the Sabbath" (Mark 2:28). To Peter and his fellow apostles, Jesus asked this searching question: "Whom do men say that I the Son of man am?" Speaking by the Spirit, Peter answered, "Thou art the Christ, the Son of the living God" (Matt. 16:13-16).

Concerning our Lord saying he is the Son of Man, Elder Bruce R. McConkie explains, "that this exalted name/title has a deep and glorious connotation . . . *Its greatest significance lies in the fact that it identifies and reveals who the Father is.*

"In the early dispensations, the Father revealed many of his names. 'Behold, *I am God*; *Man of Holiness* is my name: *Man of Counsel* is my name; and *Endless and Eternal* is my name, also,' he said to Enoch" (Moses 7:35). Revealing other names, our apostolic scholar says that "another of his names is '*Righteousness*,' or, perhaps better, '*Man of Righteousness*.' In other words, to signify that he is the personification and embodiment of those godly attributes which men must obtain if they are to be one with him, he takes these attributes as his names. Thus we read that it was said to the first man: 'In the language of Adam, *Man of Holiness is his name*, and the name of his Only Begotten is the *Son of Man*, even Jesus Christ, a righteous Judge, who shall come in the meridian of time' (Moses 6: 57).

"That is, the Father is a Holy Man. Man of Holiness is his name, and the name of his Only Begotten is the Son of Man of Holiness, or in its abbreviated form, the Son of Man."[42]

Due to the fact that Elder McConkie has written more on the names of the Father than any General Authority, his words will be quoted frequently in this chapter. With this stated, we continue with the name-titles of the Father.

MAN OF COUNSEL

As has been mentioned, another revealed name of the Father is *Man of Counsel* (Moses 7:35). This designation signifies he is a "Man and that the perfection of counsel and direction come from him." In a "similar manner, he might be called *Man of Wisdom, Man of Righteousness, Man of Power, Man of Love,* or any other name-title which points attention to the perfection and beauty of a particular one of the godly attributes embodied in his Person."[43]

MAN OF RIGHTEOUSNESS

Since Christ is the *Son of Righteousness* (2 Ne. 26:9; 3 Ne. 25:2; Ether 9:22), it follows that God his Father is named *Righteousness*. Accordingly, another exalted name of the Father is *Man of Righteousness*; which compliments his other names: *Man of Counsel* and *Man of Holiness*. This is in keeping with the general principle whereunder members of the Godhead reveal themselves under names which point men's attention to characteristics and attributes which are perfected in Deity. Thus God being the embodiment of righteousness chooses that as a name for himself to certify such trust to his children on earth. In like manner he might call himself *Wisdom, Love, Power, Counsel, Faith*, or a great number of such types of names.[44]

AHMAN

For reasons of his own, the Prophet Joseph Smith never recorded every revelation he received from the Lord. Fortunately for us, one of these was related by Elder Orson Pratt. In a marvelous discourse delivered in the open air, on the Temple Block in Salt Lake City, February 18, 1855, he said:

> There is one revelation that this people are not generally acquainted with. I think it has never been published, but probably will be in the Church History. It is given in questions and answers. The first question is, "What is the name of God in the pure language [spoken by Adam]?" The answer says, "*Ahman*." "What is the name of the Son of God?" Answer, "*Son Ahman* . . ." "What is the name of men?" "*Sons Ahman*," is the answer. "What is the name of angels in the pure language?" "*Anglo-man*."[45]

With additional insight on this subject, Elder McConkie says: "In the pure language spoken by Adam—and which will be spoken again during the millennium era (Zeph. 3: 9)—the name of God the Father is *Ahman*, or possibly *Ah Man*, a name-title having a meaning identical with or at least very closely akin to *Man of Holiness* (Moses 6:57). God revealed himself to Adam by this name to signify that he is a *Holy Man*, a truth which man must know and comprehend if he is to become like God and inherit exaltation (1 John 3:1-3; D & C 132:19-24)."[46]

ALMIGHTY GOD

Both the Father and the Son are described in scriptures as "*Almighty* (Gen 49:25; Rev. 1:8; 2 Ne. 23:6; Helaman 10: 11; D&C 84: 96; 121: 33); *Almighty God* (Gen. 17:1; 28:3; 1 Ne. 17: 48; D&C 20:21; 87:6; 88: 106); *Lord Almighty* (D&C 84: 118; 2 Cor. 6: 18); and *Lord God Almighty* (Rev. 4:8; 11: 17; 21:22; D&C 109:77; 121; 4: 1 Ne. 1:14; 2 Ne. 9:46, Italics added). These designations signify that these holy beings have all power and unlimited might. A deep sense of reverence is implicit in the use of each name-title."[47]

CREATOR

Reiterating what has been written in Chapter 2, we are informed from teachings given by the Prophet Joseph Smith, along with various scriptures written, that three, separate individuals comprise the Godhead—The Father, Son, and Holy Ghost. According to Abraham's record, they are known as *God the first, the Creator*; God the second, the Redeemer; and God the third, the witness or Testator. Accordingly, we are informed of specific roles within the Godhead. As such, we know that God the Father is the supreme member of the Godhead, for he is the Creator.

Though we are informed of specific roles within the Godhead, both the Father and Son are designated as the *Creator* (Moses 1; 2; 3; *Teachings of the Prophet Joseph Smith*, p. 190). Under the direction of the Father, the Son created the earth we live upon.

Though the Father and Son have similar attributes, there are two creative events which are exclusively the Father's: "First, he is the Father of all spirits, Christ's included; none were fathered or created by anyone else. Second, he is the Creator of the physical body of man. Though Jehovah and Michael and many of the noble and great ones played their assigned roles in the various creative events, yet when it came time to place man on earth, the Lord God [who is the Father] himself performed the creative acts. 'I, God, created man in mine own image, in the image of mine Only Begotten created I him; male and female created I them'" (Moses 2:27).[48]

ELOHIM

"The name *Elohim* is of frequent occurrence in the Hebrew texts of the Old Testament," says Elder James E. Talmage, "though it is not found in our English version. In form the word is a Hebrew plural noun; but it connotes the plurality of excellence or intensity, rather than distinctively of number. It is expressive of supreme or absolute exaltation and power. *Elohim*, as understood and used in the restored Church of Jesus Christ, is the name-title of God the Eternal Father, whose firstborn Son in the spirit is Jehovah—the Only Begotten in the flesh, Jesus Christ."[49]

Providing further information, Elder McConkie explains: "*Elohim* is the plural of the Caanite *El* or the Hebrew *Eloah*; consequently, its literal meaning is Gods. Accordingly, as the Prophet pointed out, such Old Testament passages as, 'In the beginning God (Elohim) created the heaven and earth' (Gen.

1:1), should more properly be translated, 'In the beginning *the head of the Gods* brought forth the Gods,' and they created the heavens and earth."[50]

As is apparent, most of the name-titles of the Father equally apply to the Son. However, it is highly significant that the Son is never called by this particular name—Elohim. This unique name specifically means the *Father*—for he is the head of the Gods, as far as it pertains to our Godhead members.

ENDLESS AND ETERNAL

Combining these words as though they are one, the Lord said to Enoch that "*Endless and Eternal* is my name" (Moses 7:35). "*Endless*, used as a noun and not as an adjective, is one of the names of God and signifies his unending, eternal continuance as the supreme, exalted ruler of the universe. 'Behold, I am the Lord God Almighty, and *Endless* is my name,' he said, 'for I am without beginning of days or end of years; and is not this endless?' (Moses 1: 3: 7: 35). '*Endless* is my name' he said to the Prophet" (D&C 19: 10).[51]

"One of the names of God is *Eternal*; to Enoch the Lord said, 'Eternal is my name' (Moses 7:35), using this designation as a noun and not as an adjective. This name of Deity signifies that he is 'infinite and eternal, from everlasting to everlasting, the same unchangeable God.' (D&C 20:17) In fact, members of the godhead, possessing the same characteristics and attributes are 'infinite and eternal, without end.' (D&C 20:28, 77, 79; 121:32; 128:23). Later in his writings, he says, '*Eternal* is also used to mean the opposite of *temporal*, the opposite of that which pertains to *time* and *mortality*.'"[52]

From these expressions, we can better understand why the Father combined one of his name-titles as Endless and Eternal. (Moses 7:35) It is very descriptive of the type of being he is.

FATHER

Likewise, both the Father and the Son are called *Father*. Concerning the first member of the Godhead, he is also called our *Eternal Father*, *Father in Heaven*, *Heavenly Father*, and *Holy Father*. "God the Eternal Father, our *Father in Heaven*, is an exalted, perfected, and glorified Personage having a tangible body of flesh and bones (D&C 130:22). The designation *Father* is to be taken literally; it signifies that the Supreme Being is the literal Parent or Father of spirits of all men (Heb. 12:9). All men, Christ included, were born as his children in pre-existence (D&C 93:21-23; Moses 1; 2; 3; 4; Abra. 3:22-28). This is the reason men are commanded to approach Deity in prayer by saying, 'Our Father which art in heaven'" (Matt. 6:9).

Speaking of the *Fatherhood of God* and the *Brotherhood of Man*, our apostolic scholar points out that our "Lord had reference to this when he said [to Mary], 'Go to my brethren, and say unto them, I ascend unto my Father, and your Father; and to my God, and your God'" (John 20:17).[53]

GOD

As has been previously explained, each member of the Godhead is called a *God*. "By definition, God, (generally meaning the Father) is the supreme and absolute Being."[54] The Prophet Joseph Smith observed "that God is the only supreme governor and independent Being in whom all fulness and perfection dwell; who is omnipotent, omnipresent, and omniscient; without beginning of days or end of life; and that in him every good gift and every good principle dwell; and the he is the Father of lights; in him the principle of faith dwells independently, and he is the object in whom the faith of all other rational and accountable beings centers for life and salvation."[55]

Specifically speaking of the Father, Elder McConkie further

says, "Man's purpose in life is to learn the nature and kind of being that God is, and then, by conformity to his laws and ordinances, to progress to that high state of exaltation wherein man becomes perfect as the Father is perfect' (Matt. 5:48; *Teachings*, pp. 342-362).[56]

HIGHEST

"To the Father, 'the highest of all' (D&C 76:70), is ascribed the name, the *Highest* (Ps. 87:5; Luke 1:32-35, 76; 2:14; 6:35; 19:38), thus signifying that he is exalted above all others in standing, rank, dignity, power, and all things. Of the Father, he who is 'the Son of the Highest' (Luke 1:32) proclaimed: 'My Father is greater than I'" (John 14:28).[57]

IMMANENT GOD

The Father and the Son are called an *Immanent God.* This name means each are the "indwelling Presence in all immensity. ' In him we live, and move, and have our being.' (Acts 17:28) 'He is above all things, and in all things, and is round about all things; and all things are by him, and of him, even God, forever and ever.' (D&C 88:41) . . .

"God himself, of course, is a personal Being in whose image man is created . . . but he is also an immanent Being, meaning that the light of Christ shines forth from him to fill all space. This 'light proceedeth forth from the presence of God to fill the immensity of space—The light which is in all things, which giveth life to all things, which is the law by which all things are governed, even the power of God *who sitteth upon his throne, who is in the bosom of eternity, who is in the midst of all things*'" (D&C 88: 12-13).[58]

LORD

Both the Father and the Son are commonly referred to as *Lord*. "Embraced within this appellation is the concept that they are supreme in authority and sovereign over all, that they are the rulers and governors of all things" (Psalms 110:1; Matt. 22:41-46). "By uniting the sacred names *Lord* and *God* into such reverential combinations as *God the Lord* or *Lord God* (Moses 3:4), superlative expression is made of the majesty, omnipotence, and glory of Deity. These names—used, as the various scriptural contexts show, with reference to both the Father and the Son—are also sometimes expanded to be, among others: *Lord God of Abraham* (Gen. 28:13), *Lord God of Israel* (Ex. 32: 27), *Lord God of Elijah* (2 Kings 2:14), *Lord God of our Fathers* (2 Chron. 20:6), *Lord God of hosts*, (1 Kings 19:10), and *Lord God Almighty"* (Rev. 4:8; 11:17; 15:3; 16:7; D&C 109:77; 121:4).[59]

Further, both the "Father and the Son are properly known by the title *Lord of Lords*. A designation that means literally what it says" (Deut. 10: 12-22; 1 Tim. 6:15; Rev. 17:14; 19:16)[60] (Italics added).

MOST HIGH

In addition, both the Father and the Son bear the name the Most High. (Deut. 32: 8-9; Isa. 14:4; Mark 5:7; D&C 36:3; 39:19; 76:57) "This designation connotes a state of supreme exaltation in rank, power, and dignity; it indicates that each of these Gods is God above all. Obviously the Father is the Most High God in the literal sense for he is the God of the Son as well as the God of all men. (John 20:17) The Son, however, is the Most High God in the sense that by divine investiture of authority, he is endowed with the power and authority of the Father, speaks in his name as though he were the Father, and therefore (having the fulness of the Father) he thinks it 'not robbery to be equal with God'" (Philip 2:6).[61]

In a sermon given at the Salt Lake Tabernacle, on April 9, 1852, President Brigham Young said: "Our God and Father in Heaven, is a being of tabernacle, or, in other words, He has a body, with parts the same as you and I have . . . His Son Jesus Christ has become a personage of tabernacle, and has a body like his Father . . . ."[62]

From all of the exalted name-titles presented in this chapter, it signifies that our Heavenly Father is a *personal and living God*, and the personification and embodiment of these godly attributes. Our glorious goal is to become like him!

5

GOD THE FATHER IS A HEAVENLY PARENT—
HEAVENLY FATHER

Returning to the Intercessory Prayer given by our Lord, wherein he prayed: "And this is life eternal, that they might know thee the only true God, and Jesus Christ, whom thou hast sent" (John 17:3). In order to know the Father, it is necessary to believe that he is the Heavenly Parent of all the spirits of mankind. The thought of God as our Father is a principle of the gospel that generates an assurance that he cares for each of his children in a personal and loving way. Though our memories have a veil of forgetfulness placed upon them, it is equally necessary to believe that we lived with our Heavenly Father for a long time and are acquainted with him and have a close parent and child relationship.

President Brigham Young declared: "It is one of the first principles of the doctrine of salvation to become acquainted with our Father and our God. The Scriptures teach that this is eternal life, to 'know Thee, the only true God, and Jesus Christ whom thou hast sent;' this is as much as to say that no man can enjoy or be prepared for eternal life without that knowledge . . .

THE ETERNAL FATHER AND HIS SON

"I want to tell you, each and every one of you, that you are well acquainted with God our Heavenly Father, or the great Elohim. *You are all well-acquainted with Him, for there is not a soul of you but what has lived in His house and dwelt with Him year after year; and yet you are seeking to become acquainted with Him, when the fact is, you have merely forgotten* [due to the veil of forgetfulness] *what you did know.*

"There is not a person here to-day (sic) but what is a son or a daughter of that Being. *In the spirit world their spirits were first begotten and brought forth, and they lived there with their parents for ages before they came here* [to this earth] . . ."[63]

As to what will happen when we are worthy to return to the presence of the Father, we again use the words of President Young: "To you who are prepared to enter into the presence of the Father and the Son, what I am now telling will eventually be no more strange than are the feelings of a person who returns to his father's house, brethren, and sisters, and enjoys the society of his old associates, after an absence of several years upon some distant island. Upon returning he would be happy to see his father, his relatives and friends. *So also if we keep the celestial law when our spirits go to God who gave them, we shall find that we are acquainted there and distinctly realize that we know all about that world.*[64]

In another discourse, President Young continued this teaching: "The generality of mankind are ignorant of the real relationship that exists between them and Heaven. *They do not understand that God is our Father.*" Asking a question of the congregation, he said: "By adoption?" Answering his own question, he replied: "No; but *we are his children by legal inheritance.*" To help the congregation understand the close relationship we have with the Father and the Son, he explained: "When you approach the throne of grace and petition the Father [in prayer], in the name of that Saviour who has redeemed the world, *do you use that name as the name of a stranger? If you understand your own religion, you petition that Personage as you would one of your brethren in the flesh.* Is this strange to you? It should bring near to you things that pertain to eternity, give your reflections and views a more exalted cast, stamp your daily actions with truth and honesty, and cause you to be filled with the Spirit and power of God."[65]

Sometimes members of the Church lose sight of the fact that when they say prayers, they are speaking to a personal and loving Father. Likewise, they lose sight that he knows each of us by name, and he wants us to speak to him openly, honestly, and with faith.

Concerning the doctrine that God the Father is a Heavenly Parent, Bishop Orson F. Whitney stated: ". . . He is the Creator of all things—the maker of the earth, the maker of heaven, *and that the children of men are the sons and daughters of one common parentage*; that He feels for them all the day long; that He has their welfare constantly in view, and He makes no movement, so far as His children upon this earth are concerned, but He does it for their salvation and their good here and hereafter."[66]

Because of the veil of forgetfulness placed on our minds, many people wander aimlessly in life with no knowledge that they are a spirit child of a loving and caring Father in Heaven. This is why missionary work in the Church is so vital and important; to teach the world that they are a child of God, and that he has a plan that allows them an opportunity to come back into his presence, and become like him. With this stated, we again use the words of Bishop Whitney:

"We are placed in this world measurably in the dark. We no longer see our Father face to face. While it is true that we once did; that we once stood in His presence . . .; the curtain has dropped, we have changed our abode, we have taken upon ourselves flesh; the vail [sic] of forgetfulness intervenes between this life and that, and we are left, as Paul expresses it, to 'see through a glass darkly,' to 'know in part and to prophesy in part;' to see only to a limited extent, the end from the beginning. We do not comprehend things in their fullness. But we have the promise, if we will receive and live by every word that proceeds from the mouth of God, wisely using the intelligence, the opportunities, the advantages, and the possessions which He continually bestows upon us—the time will come, in the eternal course of events, when our minds will be cleared from every cloud, the past will recur to memory, the future will be an open vision, and we will behold things as they are, and the past, present, and future will be one eternal day, as it is in the eyes of God our Father . . .; whose course is one eternal round; who creates, who saves, redeems and glorifies the workmanship of His hands, in which He Himself is glorified." Later in his discourse, he declared: "Thus it is that the Latter-day Saints preach the everlasting Gospel, the unchangeable way of eternal life . . ."[67]

HEAVENLY MOTHER

Logic leads us to the fact that our Father in Heaven is not a Single Parent. As Bishop Whitney has aptly stated, "the children of men are the sons and daughters of one common parentage."[68] That *common parentage is our Heavenly Parents.*

One of the great thinkers in the Church was Elder Orson Pratt. Combing scripture and reason, he expressed the following thoughts: "If none but Gods will be permitted to multiply immortal children, it follows that each God must have one or more wives. God, the Father of our spirits, became the Father of our Lord Jesus Christ, according to the flesh. Hence, the Father saith concerning him, 'Thou art my Son, this day have I begotten thee.'"

Later in his writing, he says: "As God the Father begat the fleshly body of Jesus, so He, before the world began, begat his spirit. As the body required an earthly Mother, so his spirit required a heavenly Mother. As God associated in the capacity of a husband with the earthly mother, so likewise He associated in the same capacity with the heavenly one." Specifically speaking of our Mother in Heaven, he asks this question: "But if we have a heavenly Mother as well as a heavenly Father, is it not right that we should worship the Mother of our spirits as well as the Father?" Answering his own question, he says: "No; for the Father of our spirits is at the head of His household, and His wives and children are required to yield the most perfect obedience to their great Head . . .

"Although she [our Mother in Heaven] is highly exalted and honored as the beloved bride of the great King, yet the children, so far as we are informed, have never been commanded to pray to her or worship her. Jesus prayed to His Father, and taught His disciples to do likewise; but we are nowhere taught that Jesus prayed to His Heavenly Mother . . ."[69]

Concerning the doctrine of a Heavenly Father and Mother, Elder Erastus Snow said: "Now, it is not said in so many words in the Scriptures, *that we have a Mother in Heaven as well as a Father*. It is left for us to infer this from what we see and know of all living things in the earth including man. The male and female principle is united and both necessary to the accomplishment of the object of their being . . .

"Hence when it is said that God created our first parents in His Likeness—'in the image of God created He him; male and female created he them;' It is intimated in language sufficiently plain to my understanding *that the male and female principle was present with the Gods as it is with man . . .*"[70]

Providing additional information on this glorious doctrine of a Heavenly Mother, Elder Bruce R. McConkie says: "Implicit in the Christian verity that all men are the spirit children of an *Eternal Father* is the usually unspoken truth that they are also the offspring of an *Eternal Mother*. An exalted and glorified Man of Holiness (Moses 6: 57) could not be a Father unless a Woman of like glory, perfection, and holiness was associated with him as a Mother. The begetting of children makes a man a father and a woman a mother whether we are dealing with man in his mortal or immortal state.

"This doctrine that there is a *Mother in Heaven* was affirmed in plainness by the First Presidency of the Church (Joseph F. Smith, John R. Winder, and Anthon H. Lund) when, in speaking of premortal existence and the origin of man, they said that 'man, as a spirit, was begotten and born of *heavenly parents*, and reared to maturity in the eternal mansions of the Father,' that man is the 'offspring of *celestial parentage*,' and that 'all men and women are in the similitude of the universal Father and Mother, and are literally the sons and daughters of deity'" (*Man: His Origin and Destiny*, pp. 348-355).[71]

Referring to a hymn that is sung often in our meetings, Elder McConkie continues: "This glorious truth of celestial parentage, including specifically both a Father and a Mother, is heralded forth by song in one of the greatest of Latter-day Saint hymns. *O My Father* by Eliza R. Snow, written in 1843, during the lifetime of the Prophet, includes this teaching:

> In the heavens are parents single?
> No; the thought makes reason Stare!
> Truth is reason, truth eternal,
> Tells me I've a Mother there.
>
> When I leave this frail existence,
> When I lay this mortal by,
> Father, Mother, may I meet you
> In your royal courts on high?
>
> Then, at length, when I've completed
> All you sent me forth to do,
> With your mutual approbation,
> Let me come and dwell with you.[72]

BECOMING LIKE OUR HEAVENLY PARENTS

The basic unit in the Church is the family. Generally speaking, a family consists of a father, mother, and children. This glorious pattern was vividly portrayed in the premortal existence; all of the spirit sons and daughters were born of one common parentage—our Heavenly Parents.

"Mortal persons," says Elder McConkie, "who overcome all things and gain an ultimate exaltation will live eternally in the family unit and have spirit children, thus becoming Eternal Fathers and Eternal Mothers. (D&C 132:19-32) Indeed, the formal pronouncement of the Church, issued by the First Presidency and the Council of the Twelve, states: 'So far as the stages of eternal progression and attainment have been made known through divine revelation, we are to understand that *only resurrected and glorified beings can become parents of spirit offspring*'" (Man: His Origin and Destiny, p.129).[73]

Whether sacred ordinances performed in the temples are for the living or the dead, it allows individuals the opportunity to live eternally in a family unit. The purpose of the Church is to put families together, not pull them apart. As Elder McConkie further says, "Those who gain eternal life (exaltation) also gain eternal lives, meaning that in the resurrection they have eternal 'increase,' 'a continuation of the seeds,' 'a continuation of the lives.'"[74]

Because our Heavenly Parents live in an eternal family unit, our glorious goal is to become like our beloved Heavenly Father and Mother.

6

ADAM: A SON OF GOD THE FATHER—
WRITINGS OF ABRAHAM AND MOSES

God the Father is the Heavenly Parent of billions of spirit sons and daughters who come to this world. In addition, he is the Father of three children who have had physical bodies on this earth: Adam; his wife Eve, and our Savior, Jesus Christ. Regarding the ability of our Father in Heaven to produce both spirit bodies and physical bodies for his children, President Brigham Young revealed the following doctrine: "We [mortals on earth] have not the power in the flesh to create and bring forth or produce a spirit; but we have the power to produce a temporal body [meaning a mortal child]. The germ of this, God has placed within us. And when our spirits receive our bodies [at the resurrection], and through our faithfulness we are worthy to be crowned [a god], we will then receive authority to produce both spirit and body."[75]

Contrary to teachings expounded in many scientific writings, we are informed by the Lord, himself, that *"the first man of all men have I called* Adam, which is many." (Moses 1:34; 3:7; 6:45; Abraham 1:3; 1 Ne. 5:11; D&C 84:16, italics added).

This means that Adam was the first of the human family on this earth and his name means *many*, signifying the greatness of his posterity.

Concerning Adam and Eve, we turn to the Book of Genesis and read these words:

"And God said, Let us make man in our image, after our likeness . . . So God created man in his own image, in the image of God created he him; male and female created he them" (1:26-27).

Therefore, Adam was created in the image of God the Eternal Father; Eve was created in the image of her Eternal Mother in Heaven. Likewise, all of mankind is created in the image of our Eternal Heavenly Parents.

As it pertains to Adam only, the First Presidency of the Church (Joseph F. Smith, John R. Winder, Anthon H. Lund) have written: "Adam, our great progenitor, 'the first man,' was, like Christ, a pre-existent spirit, and like Christ he took upon him an appropriate body, the body of a man, and so became a 'living soul' . . . and that all who have inhabited the earth since Adam have taken bodies and become souls in like manner. Man began life as a human being, *in the likeness of our heavenly father* . . ."[76]

In harmony with this statement, the Lord revealed the following to the Prophet Joseph Smith: ". . . *that which is spiritual being in the likeness of that which is temporal*; and that which is temporal in the likeness of that which is spiritual; *the spirit of man in the likeness of his person*, as also the spirit of the beast, and every other creature which God has created" (D&C 77:2, italics added).

Since Adam and Eve, as well as all of mankind, are patterned after their spirit body, the two look so much alike that if we were to see both of them standing side by side, we could not tell them apart by looking at them. Likewise, being patterned after their Heavenly Parents, Adam and Eve were created in the image and likeness of their Heavenly Father and Mother.

HOW ADAM WAS FORMED

Both accounts written in the *Pearl of Great Price* says that "God," but more correctly "the Gods" (meaning: Our Father in Heaven and a Heavenly Mother) "formed man from the dust of the ground . . ." (Abraham 5:7 and Moses 3:7). These scriptures have raised questions concerning how Adam was formed. Some have supposed that God the Father literally formed him from the dust of this earth.

For a wise reason, the scriptures have not provided the personal details of how Adam was formed. Spiritual knowledge is gained by study and by prayer. Many people in the world are neither prepared nor willing to accept the teachings expounded in The Church of Jesus Christ of Latter-day Saints. Even some members of the Church say that Adam's formation is a mystery of the gospel. To those who are prepared to receive spiritual knowledge, the Lord has declared:

"If thou shalt ask thou shalt receive revelation upon revelation, knowledge upon knowledge, that thou mayest know the mysteries and peaceable things—that which bringeth joy, that which bringeth life eternal . . . For unto you it is given to know the mysteries of the kingdom, but not unto the world, it is not given to know them" (D&C 42: 62-65; 6:7, 11; 8:11; 11:7).

In conjunction with this scripture, the following truth is stated: "Surely the Lord God will do nothing, but he revealeth his secret unto his servants the prophets" (Amos 3:7).

With these scriptures presented, let us learn how Adam was formed. Logic should lead us to the fact that Adam was not formed from dirt and clay, but that he was formed through the process of procreation and birth. In support of these statements, the First Presidency wrote the following letter:

"Salt Lake City, UTAH
February 20, 1912
President Samuel O. Bennion
Independence, Missouri

Dear Brother:

Your question concerning Adam has not been answered because of pressure of important business . . .

If you will carefully examine the sermon to which you refer . . . you will discover that . . . President [Brigham] Young denied that Jesus was 'begotten by the Holy Ghost' . . .

President Young went on to show that our father Adam—that is, our earthly father—the progenitor of the race of man, stands at the head, being 'Michael the Archangel, the Ancient of Days,' and *that he was not fashioned from earth like an adobe, but was begotten by his Father in Heaven.*

Your brethren,
Joseph F. Smith
Anthon H. Lund
Charles W. Penrose, First Presidency.[77]

Besides this statement, the Prophet Joseph Smith declared: *"Where was there ever a son without a father?* And where was there ever a father without first being a son? Wherever did a tree or anything spring into existence without a progenitor? And everything comes in this way."[78]

In discussing the principle of procreation as the process by which life was organized initially on earth, President Joseph F. Smith said:

"The Son, Jesus Christ, grew and developed into manhood the same as you or I, as likewise did God, his Father, grow and developed to the Supreme Being that He now is. Man was born of woman; Christ, the Savior, was born of woman; and God, the

THE ETERNAL FATHER AND HIS SON

Father, was born of woman. *Adam, our earthly parent, was also born of woman into this world, the same as Jesus and you and I."*[79]

In addition to this statement, in a course of study for the Church, entitled *The Divine Mission of the Savior*, the following was written:

"The Creation of Adam and Eve—One of the important points about the topic is to learn, if possible, how Adam obtained his body of flesh and bones. There would seem to be but one natural and reasonable explanation, and that is, that Adam obtained his body in the same way Christ obtained his— and just as all men obtain theirs—*namely, by being born of woman."*[80]

Combining the above statements, it is evident that Adam had a Father as well as a Mother. In addition, that he was born of woman on this earth, the identical way that all men and women are born in mortality.

Many individuals have wondered if Adam had a navel. Based on the statement that he was born of woman, the answer is affirmative. Concerning his birth process, and supporting the fact that he was not formed from dust as an adobe, the First Presidency wrote the following statement:

"True it is that the body of man enters upon its career as a tiny germ or embryo, which becomes an infant, quickened at a certain stage by the spirit whose tabernacle it is, and the child, after being born, develops into a man. *There is nothing in this, however, to indicate that the original man, the first of our race, began life as anything less than a man, or less than the human germ or embryo that becomes a man.'"*[81]

Based on this information, it is reasonable to believe that God the Father came down to this earth, after its creation, with an exalted Wife, and through a literal union, they conceived a child. At the appointed time, this child was born of woman, and he grew up and become known as Adam. The Father and his exalted Wife did the same and brought forth a girl, who grew up and became Eve. As such, Adam and Eve had bodies of flesh and bones, but were not mortal, not until they fell. Likewise, Adam and Eve were not translated beings; nor were they resurrected beings and transported here from another world! But, their spirits came here from premortal existence like all who have been born on this earth. God the Father and a Mother in Heaven created their bodies on this earth. As such, Adam and Eve are the physical children of Heavenly Parents.

ADAM AND EVE BORN IMMORTAL

Elder Bruce R. McConkie has said: "Christ is the *Son of God*; and he has been so designated from the beginning to show the personal, intimate, family relationship that exists between him and his Father . . .

"Father Adam, the first man, is also a *son of God* (Luke 3:38; Moses 6:22, 59), a fact that does not change the great truth that Christ is the Only Begotten in the flesh, for *Adam's entrance into this world was in immortality*. He came here before death had its beginning . . . with its consequent mortal or flesh-status of existence."[82]

Because God the Father and his Eternal Companion can *produce both spirit bodies and physical bodies*, Adam is a *son of God*, the same as Jesus Christ is a *Son of God*. The difference is that Adam [and we must add Eve also] *were born immortal*, upon this earth, from God the Father and a Mother in Heaven. Jesus Christ was born mortal, upon this earth, from God the Father and the mortal woman, Mary.

Giving us additional insight on Adam and Eve, Elder McConkie has further written that "Adam . . . the first man, was the first of the earth's inhabitants to see the Lord. He and his wife, Eve, had intimate and extended association with both the Father and the Son before the fall and while they dwelt in

THE ETERNAL FATHER AND HIS SON

Eden's hallowed vales (Moses 3 and 4). *They then knew, before mortality entered the world, that they were the offspring of Exalted Parents in whose image they were made.* It was as automatic and instinctive for them to know their ancestry, their family relationship, and the exalted destiny they might obtain, as it is for mortal children to grow and assume they will be like their parents."[83]

All of mankind is a spiritual son or daughter of God the Father; thereby making all of us spiritual brother and sisters. As it pertains to Adam and Eve and our Savior, Jesus Christ, *that family relationship extends more than spiritual.* Eve is the body sister to Adam and our Savior. Adam and our Savior are body brothers; the same as they are with their sister Eve. While in the Garden of Eden, Adam and Eve conversed with their resurrected and exalted Father, and their spirit-body Brother, who would eventually become the mortal Savior on this earth. As has been explained, Adam and Eve are body children of God the Father and a Mother in Heaven; and each were born immortal on this earth, with no blood flowing in their veins, until after they fell. Our Savior is also the body child of God the Father. The distinctive difference between the birth of Adam and Eve and our Savior is that our Savior's mother was a mortal woman.

7

MARY AND GOD THE FATHER—
MARY AND EVE

As has been explained in the previous chapter, our Savior is the body child of God the Father and the mortal woman, Mary. To help us understand why our Savior's birth was different than that of Adam's and Eve's, it will be helpful to learn more about the role of Mary in this unique family relationship.

It was necessary that the mortal mother of Jesus Christ be born at a certain time and certain geographical location. By divine providence, she was raised a Jew, in the city of Nazareth of Galilee, 2,000 years ago, and took upon herself physical features similar to her premortal spirit (Matt. 2:23; Luke 1:26-30; 1 Ne. 11:13; D& C 77:2).[84]

Due to her valiancy in keeping the teachings and commandments of God, Mary was selected above all the female spirits assigned to this earth and foreordained to become the mortal mother of Jesus Christ. Concerning her spiritual status, we use the words of Elder Bruce R. McConkie:

> Can we speak too highly of her whom the Lord has blessed above all women? There was only one Christ,

THE ETERNAL FATHER AND HIS SON

and there is only one Mary. Each was noble and great in the premortal existence and each was foreordained to the ministry he or she performed. We cannot but think that the Father would choose the greatest female spirit to be the mother of his Son, even as he chose the male spirit like unto him to be the Savior . . . [85]

In view of Eve being the first woman on earth, and the mother of all living (Moses 4:26; 1 Ne.5:11), and Mary being the mother of our Lord, we may wonder who of the two was the greater in the premortal life? To answer this question, we again rely upon the wisdom and logic Elder McConkie:

"In my judgment, Mary is the number one woman who has ever lived on earth; she is the spirit daughter of God our Father, who was chosen to provide a body for his Son, who was born after the manner of the flesh . . .

> I rate Eve as the number two woman among all of those who have or will come to earth. She, as the mother of all living, set the pattern for all future mothers with reference to bringing up their children in light and truth. She received all of the blessings of the gospel, enjoyed the gifts of the Spirit, and sought to prepare her posterity for like blessings . . . Now, from this point there is no order of priority. I have no reservation in acclaiming Mary as the number one woman of the earth and Eve as the number two. [86]

It needs to be emphasized that Mary came into this world bringing with her the talents, gifts, abilities, and spiritual endowments that she earned in abundance and developed in the premortal existence.

After this Jewish maiden was born on earth, her parents gave her the name that was revealed years earlier to holy men of God. That special name was Mary (Mosiah 3:8; Alma 7:10).

Her earthly parents cared and provided for her temporal and spiritual needs. As Mary grew, she was taught to be mannerly, well-groomed, virtuous, and a responsible and productive person. Further, this Jewish maiden was taught the Law of Moses, as well as the prophecies of the Promised Messiah. Because of her domestic and religious training in the home, Mary believed in God, had faith and religious hope in his teachings, and lived his holy commandments. With a combination of her premortal nature, and the religious training she received in mortality, Mary rapidly learned the commandments of God and willingly conformed her life accordingly. Mary truly was a precious and chosen vessel (Alma 7:10).

GABRIEL'S VISIT

The scriptural record is silent on the day and time that this heavenly manifestation transpired. What we do know is that while alone in the home of her parents, Mary was visited by a heavenly messenger from God, by the name of Gabriel. From the Prophet Joseph Smith, we learn that Gabriel was known in mortality as Noah. [87]

In her home, and with respect, the angel declared, "Hail, thou that art highly favoured, the Lord is with thee: *blessed art thou among women.*

"And when she saw him, she was troubled at his saying, and cast in her mind what manner of salutation this should be" (Luke 1:28-29).

Is it any wonder why Mary was "troubled" by Gabriel's appearance and greeting? Knowing of her feelings and concerns, this heavenly messenger spoke these calming and informative words:

". . . Fear not, Mary: *for thou has found favour with God* [the Eternal Father].

"And, behold, thou shalt conceive in thy womb, and bring forth a son, and shalt call his name JESUS.

"He shall be great, and shall be called *the Son of the Highest* . . ." (Luke 1:30-32).

Imagine what Mary was experiencing by this heavenly manifestation. Rarely does an angel appear to individuals on earth. Then, compound this spiritual experience by the surprising announcement that she was to be the mother of the "Son of the Highest."

Regarding her response, we turn to the expressions of Elder James E. Talmage for understanding:

"Even yet she comprehended but in part the import of this momentous visitation. Not in the spirit of doubt such as had prompted Zacharias to ask for a sign, but through an earnest desire for information and explanation, Mary, conscious of her unmarried status and sure of her virgin condition, asked: 'How shall this be, seeing I know not a man?'" [88]

Gabriel, as clearly and as plainly as he could, explained to Mary:

". . . The Holy Ghost shall come upon thee, and *the power of the Highest shall overshadow thee*: therefore also that holy thing [child] which shall be born of thee shall be called the *Son of God*" (Luke 1:35).

Mary responded with gentle submissiveness and humble acceptance, ". . . Behold the handmaid of the Lord; be it unto me according to thy word" (Luke 1:38). The record states that after Mary spoke these humble and obedient words, Gabriel departed. Now alone, Mary was left to ponder, and wait, for the angel's words to be fulfilled.

We are not informed of the time between Gabriel's announcement to Mary and her entering into the presence of the Highest. All that we know is that it transpired shortly thereafter.

BRUCE E. DANA

NEPHI'S VISION OF MARY

The Lord has revealed that the premortal spirit that is housed in the mortal body is "in the likeness of that which is temporal" (D&C 77:2). Accordingly, Mary took upon herself physical characteristics that are similar to her premortal spirit.

Nearly 600 years prior to the birth of Christ, a Nephite prophet, who name is Nephi, was privileged to see Mary in vision. From this blessed man, we read of her physical attractiveness:

"For it came to pass that after I had desired to know the things my father [Lehi] had seen, and believing that the Lord was able to make them known unto me . . . I was caught away in the Spirit of the Lord, yea, into an exceedingly high mountain . . .

"And it came to pass that I looked and beheld the great city of Jerusalem, and also other cities. And I beheld the city of Nazareth; and in the city of Nazareth *I beheld a virgin, and she was exceedingly fair and white.*

". . . and the angel came down and stood before me; and he said unto me: Nephi, what beholdest thou?

"And I said unto him: *A virgin most beautiful and fair above all other virgins*" (1 Ne. 11:1-15).

According to a dictionary definition, the word *fair* means: Pleasing to the eye, flawless quality, and clean and pure. Was this not an appropriate description of Mary?

Continuing with this scriptural account, the angel told Nephi who this attractive woman was:

"And he said unto me: Behold, the virgin whom thou seest is the mother of the Son of God, *after the manner of the flesh.*" [It is worth pointing out that the angel made this comment to emphasize that our Savior's mortal mother is different than his Mother in Heaven.]

"And it came to pass that I beheld that she [Mary] was carried away in the spirit; and after she had been carried away in

THE ETERNAL FATHER AND HIS SON

the Sprit for the space of a time the angel spake unto me, saying: Look!

"And I looked and beheld the virgin again, *bearing a child in her arms*.

"And the angel said unto me: "Behold the Lamb of God, yea, *even the son of the Eternal Father!*" (1 Ne. 11:18-21, italics added).

Are we amiss to say that besides being physically attractive, Mary's personality and spiritual countenance was equally pleasing? Beauty is more than just physical. It also encompasses a variety of things such a warm personality, an unassuming and caring nature, a reverent and spiritual attitude, a special smile, honorable gestures of affection, and true goodness manifesting itself. Combining all of these traits, we may safely assume that besides being physically attractive, Mary also had a pleasing personality.

MARY WAS CARRIED AWAY IN THE SPIRIT

From Nephi, we learn an important truth regarding Mary and the conception of the Son of God. In vision, he saw that she was carried away in the Spirit; and after a time, she had a baby in her arms who was the "Son of the Eternal Father!" (1 Ne.11:18-21).

What does it mean to be carried away in the Spirit? It means to be transported bodily, by the Spirit, from one place to another. We know Nephi was bodily transported for he himself has written: "And upon the wings of his Spirit *hath my body* been carried away upon exceedingly high mountains . . ." (2 Ne. 4:25; see also Ezek. 37:1:1 Ne.1:8).

Citing the respective scriptural references, Elder McConkie has written that individually and at different times, Jesus, Ezekiel, Nephi, *Mary*, and the son of Helaman, named Nephi, and Philip were "transported bodily from place to place by the power of the Spirit." [89]

From these documented experiences, we know that within a short time after Gabriel appeared to Mary, this chosen vessel *was bodily transported* from Nazareth into *the presence of the Highest*. One moment Mary was *physically* in Nazareth; another moment she was *physically* in the presence of *God the Father*.

8

CONCEPTION OF THE SON OF GOD—
BORN OF A VIRGIN AND THE ETERNAL FATHER

Regarding Mary and the conception of the Son of God the Father, Elder James E. Talmage has written these informative words: "That child to be born of Mary was begotten of Elohim, the Eternal Father, not in violation of natural law but in accordance with a higher manifestation thereof; and, the offspring from that association of supreme sanctity, celestial Sireship, and pure though mortal maternity, was of right to be called the 'Son of the Highest.'"[90]

There are many people who do not properly understand and accept as truth that the conception of Jesus Christ was accomplished by a literal union between God the Father and the mortal Mary. With the Spirit as our guide, we will learn of doctrines that relate to this holy subject. [91]

As has been presented earlier in this work, the Father is a glorified, resurrected Man, the same as his resurrected and glorified Son (D& C 130:22). Further, the Father and the Son have a physical body similar to mortal men. Therefore, the

Highest was physically able to overshadow Mary and become the literal Father of his Son, Jesus Christ.

NATURALLY BEGOTTEN

What does it mean to be naturally begotten? To answer, we use expressions from three General Authorities. Elder Heber C. Kimball provides the following information: "I will say that I was naturally begotten; so was my father, and also my Saviour Jesus Christ. According to the Scriptures, *he is the first begotten of his father in the flesh*, and there was nothing unnatural about it."[92]

From President Brigham Young, we read: "The birth of the Saviour was as natural as are the births of our children; it was the result of natural action. He partook of flesh and blood—was begotten of *his Father*, as we are of our fathers."[93]

Elder McConkie provides this explanation: "Christ was begotten by *an Immortal Father* in the same way that mortal men are begotten by mortal fathers."[94] Our apostolic scholar further writes: "There is nothing figurative about his paternity; he was begotten, conceived and born in the normal and natural course of events, for he is *the Son of God*, and that designation means what it says."[95]

From these plainly spoken words, it should be clear that Jesus was *begotten by his Heavenly Father* in the same way that all men and women in mortality are begotten of their earthly fathers. In addition, it should be clear also that the conception of Jesus Christ was the result of a literal union between God the Father and the precious and chosen vessel, Mary.

CLARIFICATION OF MATTHEW 1:18

From the Gospel of Matthew, the following information is given: "Now the birth of Jesus Christ was on this wise: When as his mother Mary was espoused to Joseph, before they came together, she was found with child of the Holy Ghost" (Matthew 1:18).

From Matthew's account it raises doubts whether Jesus was begotten by our Heavenly Father or was the child of the Holy Ghost. To understand the meaning of Matthew's account, we again turn to Elder McConkie for explanation and clarification: "Just as Jesus is literally the Son of Mary, so *he is the personal and literal offspring of God the Eternal Father*, who himself is an exalted personage having a tangible body of flesh and bones (D&C 130:22). Apostate religionists—unable to distinguish between the father, Son, and Holy Ghost—falsely suppose that the Holy Ghost was the Father of our Lord. Matthew's statement, 'she was found with child of the Holy Ghost,' properly translated should say, 'she was found with child by the power of the Holy Ghost' (Matt. 1:18). Luke's account (Luke 1:35) accurately records what took place. Alma perfectly describes our Lord's conception and birth by prophesying: Christ 'shall be born of Mary . . . she being a virgin, a precious and chosen vessel, who shall be overshadowed and conceive by the power of the Holy Ghost, and bring forth a son, yea, even the Son of God' (Alma 7:10). Nephi spoke similarly when he said that at the time of her conception, Mary 'was carried away in the Spirit,' with the result that the child born of her was 'the lamb of God, yea, even the Son of the Eternal Father' (1 Ne. 11:19-21). As Gabriel told Luke, he was the 'Son of the Highest' (Luke 1:32), and the 'the Highest' is the first member of the godhead, not the third." [96]

From this explanation, it should be clear that *Jesus Christ is the offspring of God and Mary*; not of the Holy Ghost and Mary.

JESUS CHRIST WAS BORN OF A VIRGIN

The scriptures emphasize that Mary was a virgin. This includes the time before and after the birth of Jesus, until she was known by her husband, Joseph (Matt. 1:24-25). The question naturally arises: If indeed the Father and Mary conceived Jesus by a literal union, how can Mary remain a virgin? To answer this intriguing question, turn once again to Elder McConkie for explanation: "Mary was a virgin . . . until after the birth of our Lord. Then, for the first time, she was known by Joseph, her husband; and other children, both sons and daughters, were then born to her (Matt. 13:55-56; Mark 6:3; Gal. 1:19). She conceived and brought forth her Firstborn Son while yet a virgin because the Father of that child was an immortal personage." [97]

From this explanation, we learn that Mary's virginity was retained because of the fact that the conception of Jesus Christ was a union between a mortal woman and an *Immortal Man*. Mary ceased being a virgin when she was "known by Joseph, her husband, because that particular union was between a mortal man and mortal women." (Matt. 1:25)

JESUS CHRIST'S CONCEPTION WAS NOT DEGRADING

Some individuals may believe that if there were a literal union between the Father and Mary that this act would degrade God and debauch Mary. Elder Melvin J. Ballard gives this inspired explanation:

"Mary told the story most beautifully when she said that an angel of the Lord came to her and told her that she had found favor in the sight of God, and had come to be worthy of the fulfillment of the promises heretofore made, to become the virgin mother of the Redeemer of the world. She afterwards, referring to the event, said: 'God hath done wonderful things unto me.' 'And the Holy Ghost came upon her,' is the story, *'and she came into the presence of the highest.'* No man or woman can live in mortality and survive the presence of the *Highest* except by the sustaining power of the Holy Ghost. So it came upon her to prepare her for admittance into the divine presence, *and the*

THE ETERNAL FATHER AND HIS SON

power of the Highest, who is the Father, was present, and overshadowed her, and the holy Child that was born of her was called the *Son of God.*

"Men who deny this, or think it degrades our Father, have no true conception of the sacredness of the most marvelous power which God had endowed mortal men—the power of procreation. Even though that power may be abused and may become a mere harp of pleasure to the wicked, nevertheless it is the most sacred and holy and divine function with which God has endowed man. *Made holy, it is retained by the Father of us all,* and in his exercise of that great and marvelous creative power and function, he did not debase himself, degrade himself, nor debauch Mary. *Thus Christ became the literal Son of a divine Father, and no one else was worthy to be his father.*" [98]

From these inspired and enlightening words, we understand that mortals view the creative process differently than the Father, for as Isaiah has well written: "For my thoughts are not your thoughts, neither are your ways my ways, saith the Lord" (Isa.55:8). Elder Ballard has explained it so plainly, yet powerfully, that the creative power is the most sacred, holy, and divine function that can be performed by man and God.

Our Heavenly Father is the most holy, righteous, and pure-minded Man of all men. Further, he has the most respect for women and womanhood above all others. When Mary was in his presence and he overshadowed her, he performed a most sacred and holy function, with divine tenderness, love, and respect. Thereby, he did not degrade or debase himself or Mary.

This most righteous woman knew why she was in the Father's presence. Gabriel explained this to her while she was in Nazareth (Luke 1:35). Would we be wrong to believe that she and the Spirit communicated about sacred things while she was being bodily transported to the presence of the Highest? Further, would it be unreasonable to believe that for a short length of time the veil was taken from her mind and she was able to see the presentation of the *Father's plan of salvation* before his spirit children, as well as her own calling to be the mortal mother of Jesus Christ? Although not supported by any revealed knowledge, is there any doubt that very rapidly in the Father's presence his thoughts became her thoughts and his ways became her ways (Isa. 55:8). Further, even though Mary knew she was espoused to Joseph, the carpenter, she felt no shame, coercion, uneasiness, or hesitancy to become the mother of our Lord. This precious and chosen vessel, willing and without reservation, became the mother of Jesus Christ *because of her total love and obedience to the Father and his plan of salvation, which plan called for a Savior and Redeemer.* Accordingly, in this most sacred setting, and by their holy union, Mary conceived in her womb God's Son (Luke 1:30-32).

RELATIONSHIP OF MARY AND GOD THE FATHER

We will now present doctrines seldom mentioned, using as much propriety and plainness as possible. Regarding gospel mysteries, we shall learn of one that is the least spoken of or understood. Three General Authorities have expressed marvelous and thought-provoking comments *regarding the relationship between God the Father and Mary.* With the Spirit as our guide, let us discover what has been revealed on this holy and sacred subject.

From Elder Orson Pratt, we read these words:

> The fleshly [sic] body of Jesus required a Mother as well as a Father. Therefore, the Father and Mother of Jesus, according to the flesh, must have been associated together in the capacity of Husband and Wife; hence the *Virgin Mary must have been*, for the time being, the *lawful Wife of God the Father*: we use the term *lawful Wife*, because it would be blasphemous in the highest

degree to say that *he overshadowed her or begat the Saviour unlawfully*. It would have been unlawful for any man to have interfered with Mary, who was already espoused to Joseph; for such a heinous crime would have subjected both the guilty parties to death, according to the law of Moses. But God having created all men and women, had the most perfect right to do with his own creation, according to His holy will and pleasure: *He had a lawful right to overshadow the Virgin Mary in the capacity of a husband, and beget a Son*, although she was espoused to another; for the law which he gave to govern men and women was not intended to govern himself, or to prescribe rules for his own conduct. It was also lawful in Him, after having thus dealt with Mary, to give her to Joseph, her espoused husband. *Whether God the Father gave Mary to Joseph for time only, or for time and eternity, we are not informed. Inasmuch as God was the first husband to her*, it may be that He only gave her to be the wife of Joseph while in this mortal state, *and that He intended after the resurrection to again take her as one of his wives to raise up immortal spirits in eternity*. [99]

In the next monthly publication, Elder Pratt further wrote, "We have now clearly shown that *God the Father* had a plurality of wives, one or more being in eternity, by whom he begat our spirits as well as the spirit of Jesus His First Born, and another upon the earth by whom He begat the tabernacle of Jesus, as His Only Begotten in this world."[100]

In addition to Elder Pratt's comments, President Brigham Young stated:

"The man Joseph, the husband of Mary, did not, that we know of, have more than one wife, *but Mary the wife of Joseph had another husband* . . . that very babe that was cradled in the manger was begotten, not by Joseph, the husband of Mary, but by another being. Do you inquire by whom? *He was begotten by God our heavenly [sic] Father.*" [101]

Lastly, President Joseph F. Smith declared:

"Mary was married to Joseph for time. *No man could take her for eternity because she belonged to the Father of her divine Son.*" [102]

From these enlightening expressions, the reader will have to determine whether "the Father and Mother of Jesus, according to the flesh. . . [are] associated together in the capacity of Husband and Wife." Whatever their relationship may be, this holy and sacred event transpired exactly as Gabriel had told Mary in Nazareth:

"The Holy Ghost shall come upon thee, and the power of the Highest shall overshadow thee: therefore also that holy thing [child] which shall be born of thee shall be called the Son of God" (Luke 1:35).

In conclusion, we are not informed of the time Mary was in the presence of God our Eternal Father or what was spoken there. What we do know is that when her sacred time with the Highest was over, she was physically carried by the Spirit back to Nazareth.

With this glorious and holy experience behind her, can we begin to comprehend, even in part, what Mary has seen and experienced? Truly, as Elder Ballard pointed out: "She afterwards, referring to the event, said: 'God hath done wonderful things unto me . . .'" [103] (Luke 1:49).

From all that has been presented, we have a better understanding of the teachings concerning our Lord's conception. In addition, we have a better understanding of the unique relationship between God the Father and Mary, and how she became the mortal mother of God's Son.

9

THE FATHER AND HIS MORTAL SON—
JESUS WAS TAUGHT FROM ON HIGH

Our attention is now turned to the time of the birth of God's Only Begotten Son in the flesh (Jacob 4:5; Alma 12:33-34; D&C 20:21). Because there was no room in the inn, Mary and Joseph were staying in a manger in Bethlehem (Luke 2:7). As the Son of God, Jesus was begotten and born in the normal and natural way. Concerning our Lord's birth, Elder McConkie has appropriately written: "For the present . . . we have no way of knowing how or in what manner the Babe of Bethlehem was delivered. Was there a midwife among the travelers, who heard the cries of travail and came to Mary's aid? Did Mary alone wrap the swaddling clothes around her infant Son, or were there other hands to help? How were her needs cared for? Needless to say, the Gospel narratives are silent on these and a *lifetime of personal matters relative to the greatest life ever lived . . .*"[104]

Concerning personal matters, we have no revealed knowledge if our Heavenly Father witnessed the birth of his mortal Son, Jesus. While on this earth, the natural tendency for a father is to be with his wife and witness the birth of their son or daughter. Because of the unique relationship between Mary and the Eternal Father, we may properly assume that by his ability to see through time and space, the Father witnessed the birth of their Beloved Son (Matt. 3:17; Mark 9:10; 3 Ne.11:7; "Joseph Smith—History" 1:17).

Concerning Jesus' childhood, Elder McConkie provides this

insight: "It seems perfectly clear that our Lord grew mentally and spiritually on the same basis that he developed physically. In each case he obeyed the laws of experience and of learning and the rewards flowed to him . . . *but he was so highly endowed with talents and abilities, so spiritually sensitive, so in tune with the Infinite, that his learning and wisdom soon excelled that of all his fellows* . . .

"Further: In his study, and in the learning process, *he was guided from on high in a way that none other has ever been.* Being without sin—being clean and pure and spotless—he was entitled to the constant companionship of the Holy Spirit . . .

"With reference to Jesus' early years—those before he went to the temple at the age of twelve to discuss the doctrines of salvation with the Rabbis—Luke tells us: 'And the child grew, and waxed strong in spirit, filled with wisdom: and the grace of God was upon him'" (Luke 2:40). [105]

The special relationship between the Father and the Son is that of a *Parent and Child*. Prior to his mortal birth, our Lord was the second member in the Godhead. (*Lectures on Faith*, pp. 50-51) Jehovah, under the direction of his Father, created this earth (Colossians 1:16-17). In addition, Jesus Christ was the chosen Savior and Redeemer of the world (1 John 4:14; 1 Ne. 13:40; Alma 37:9; D&C 15:1; 43:34).

On this earth, many parents share with their younger children personal family matters. In harmony with this practice, we may safely surmise that during our Lord's "early years" that his mortal mother, Mary, told Jesus of his Father in Heaven. Likewise, Joseph, as our Lord's guardian-father, also informed Jesus of many spiritual happenings. This was one of the ways Jesus came to know his Father and their special Parent and Child relationship. However, it was *not* the only way that he came to know his Father.

Since the time of Adam to the present, prophets of God have received visions and dreams to guide them. Abraham saw "the intelligences that were organized before the world was," and he was told by God, "thou wast chosen before thou wast born" (Abraham 3:22-23).

The first Nephi mentioned in the Book of Mormon desired to know the things that his father, Lehi, had seen in vision. Believing that the Lord was able to make it known unto him, he was caught away in the Spirit, and shown the mortal mother of our Lord, carrying a child in her arms, who was the Son of the Eternal Father. Nephi further saw the baptism, ministry, and crucifixion of God's Son; as well as the calling and ministry of the twelve apostles of the Lord (1 Nephi 11:1-36). This marvelous vision was shown to Lehi and his son, Nephi, approximately 600 years before the Son of God was born in mortality.

Based on these scriptures, we wonder if the youthful Jesus were shown these same visions as Abraham and Nephi? This and a myriad of other questions might be asked of what the Boy-Jesus knew and saw.

Our attention is now turned to the expressions of Elder McConkie. In one of his books, he quotes and interjects thoughts from the writings of President J. Reuben Clark, Jr., who was a former member of the First Presidency of the Church. In speaking of what President Clark wrote, Elder McConkie penned these words: "From time to time in the course of his summary, he comes again to the concept, which seems to weigh heavily upon him, that even then, the deacon-age Jesus— scarce younger, however, than Joseph Smith, or Moroni, or Nephi, and perhaps not any younger at all than Samuel, when the Lord used these youths for his purposes—*even then he was heir to the visions of eternity on a continuing basis . . .* "[106]

He continues: "In more than a dozen instances President Clark asks whether or asserts positively that we must believe that the young Jesus—even then, and though but twelve years of age— *had past—and present vision of those things which had been in Israel and would be in the life of Israel's Chief Citizen . . .*"[107]

Though these thoughts of President Clark are highly interesting, we have no revealed knowledge that such was the case. We know that prophets have received dreams and visions to instruct them. Perhaps the youthful Jesus received dreams and visions as well? We have no revealed knowledge that he did. It only takes the Spirit to touch the memory and spiritual knowledge can be abundantly revealed. Perhaps the previous knowledge taught by the Father to Jesus in the spirit realm was revealed anew by the Spirit to the youthful Jesus? What we do know about the instruction of the God's young son is what Luke has written: "And the child grew, and *waxed strong in spirit,* filled with wisdom: *and the grace of God was upon him*" (Luke 2:40).

GOD'S SON AT AGE TWELVE

Of the four gospels, only Luke's makes mention of the Passover feast. From his record, we discover that Joseph and Mary had gone every year to Jerusalem to celebrate the Passover. (Luke 2:41) Now that Jesus was twelve years of age, it is reasonable to believe that Mary and Joseph were anxiously awaiting their yearly visit to Jerusalem. Why? To help us understand, we use the knowledge of Elder James E. Talmage:

> At twelve years of age a Jewish boy was recognized as a member of his home community; he was required then to enter with definite purpose upon his chosen profession . . . he was appointed to higher studies in school and home . . . It was the common and very natural desire of parents to have their sons attend the feast of the Passover and be present at the temple ceremonies as recognized members of the congregation when of the prescribed age. Thus came the Boy Jesus to the temple[108] (Luke 2:42).

From Luke's Gospel, we are informed that following the conclusion of the Passover stay and at the end of "a day's journey" toward Nazareth, Joseph and Mary discovered that Jesus was not with their caravan (Luke 2:44). You can imagine their shock! They immediately "turned back again to Jerusalem, seeking him." This would have taken another day. Then after still another day of searching, making it three days missing, "they found him in the temple, sitting in the midst of the doctors, both hearing them, and asking them questions." All of those who were there "were astonished at his understanding and answers" (Luke 2:44-47).

Imagine the relief of both Mary and Joseph finding Jesus alive and well, as well as the awe of hearing him conversing so impressively with the learned. We can also understand the frustration and displeasure this mother felt towards her Son when she confronted him with "Son, why hast though thus dealt with us? Behold, thy father and I have sought thee sorrowing" (Luke 2:48). The reply of their special son astonished them! Said He: "How is it that ye sought me? Wist ye not that I must be about my Father's business?" (Luke 2:49).

Though there have been different interpretations of what transpired at the temple when Jesus was twelve, it leaves us with the understanding that Jesus knew who his biological Father was. This knowledge was not obtained solely from what Mary and Joseph told him! Though we are not informed of how Jesus obtained this knowledge, we again quote the words of Elder McConkie: Jesus "was guided from on high in a way that none other has ever been." [109]

JESUS IN THE WILDERNESS WITH GOD

We now advance to a time when Jesus was thirty years of age. After his baptism by John in the river Jordan at Bethabara, we are informed from the original writings of Matthew: "Then

THE ETERNAL FATHER AND HIS SON

Jesus was led up of the Spirit, *into the wilderness, to be with God. And when he had fasted forty days and forty nights, and had communed with God*, he was afterwards an hungered, and was left to be tempted of the devil" (JST Matthew 4: 1-2, italics added). Mark's record informs us that he "was with the wild beasts; and the angels ministered unto him" (JST Mark 1: 11). As Elder McConkie has written, "Nothing more of this forty-day period is revealed . . ." [110]

From Matthew's record, we are plainly told that Jesus went into the wilderness to be with God the Father. This was an important, preparatory time for the Son of God. The following had to come from Jesus himself, for Matthew writes that during those forty days, our Lord had "communed" with his Father. Whether or not Jesus personally saw and conversed with his Father, we are not informed. We may properly assume that he prayed often to his Father; and that he earnestly tried to get close to him by having the Holy Ghost work upon him, and in his thoughts and feelings, our Lord communed with God. Someday, perhaps, the Lord will reveal how he "communed" with his Father while in the wilderness.

We know that when Jesus began his formal ministry he performed many miracles. It is noted that approximately 124 years before the birth of the Savior, a righteous Nephite king, Mosiah, revealed that our Lord "shall go forth amongst men, working mighty miracles, such as healing the sick, raising the dead, causing the lame to walk, the blind to receive their sight, and the deaf to hear, and curing all manner of diseases" (Mosiah 3:5).

How did Jesus learn to perform miracles? To answer, we again rely upon the expressions of Elder McConkie: "How do men exercise faith? If they have an occasion to heal the sick, raise the dead, or move mountains, how is it done? Faith is power, but what causes the power to flow forth and accomplish the desired result?" Then Elder McConkie quotes from *Lectures on Faith,* by the Prophet Joseph Smith, as follows: "We understand that when a man works by faith he works by *mental exertion instead of physical power. It is by words, instead of exerting his physical powers, with which every being works when he works by faith* . . . ."

Continuing, our apostolic scholar: "But working by faith is not the mere speaking of a few well-chosen words . . . *Nor is it working by faith merely a mental desire,* however strong, that some eventuality should occur . . . *only persons who are in tune with the Infinite can exercise the spiritual forces and powers that come from him* [our Lord]."

Later on, he writes: "Faith cannot be exercised contrary to the order of heaven or contrary to the will and purposes of him whose power it is. *Men work by faith when they are in tune with the Spirit and when what they seek to do by mental exertion and by the spoken word is the mind and will of the Lord.*"[111]

In this same work, Elder McConkie has penned these meaningful words: "All of these things and other miracles without number have been wrought by faith by the prophets and saints of all dispensations. *And always faith precedes the miracle; always the power of faith performs the miracle; always the miracle proves that faith was present and in active operation.*"[112]

Matthew, Mark, and John tell what happened when the apostles were in a ship on the Sea of Galilee. The soft night breeze increased into a fierce and violent wind. The length and severity of the storm had intensified the concerns and fears of all the individuals who were on the boat. When the strength of the Twelve was nearly gone, our Lord came to their rescue: "Jesus went unto them," not by land, *but by walking on the sea* (Matt. 14:22-33; Mark 6:45-52; John 6:5-6, 15-21).

How did Jesus walk on water? He had the *faith* to perform the miracle. As an adopted motto, President Heber J. Grant often quoted a saying of Ralph Waldo Emerson: "That which we persist in doing becomes easier to do, not that the nature of the thing has changed but that our power to do has increased."[113]

Would not this same principle apply to the mortal Son of God exercising faith and performing miracles? Especially when he walked on the Sea of Galilee?

While in mortality, our Lord granted that John the Beloved Apostle become a translated being (John 21:18-25; D&C 7:4-8). How did Jesus learn the doctrine of translation? As the Prophet Joseph Smith says: "Now the doctrine of translation is a power which belongs to this [the Melchizedek] Priesthood" (*Teachings of the Prophet Joseph Smith*, p. 170).

Again, the mortal Son of God had the *faith* and *authority* to perform this great miracle.

With interest, we read what Jesus told the Jews: "The Son can do nothing of himself, *but what he seeth the Father do: for what things soever he doeth, these also doeth the Son likewise. For the Father loveth the Son, and sheweth him all things that himself doeth* . . ." (John 5: 17-20, italics added). Concerning verse 20, "Sheweth him all things," Elder McConkie has written this explanation: "There is nothing which the Father has done which has not been revealed to the Son."[114]

Faith is exercised in its fullness by the Father. Therefore, based on this scripture, the Father's knowledge of *faith* was revealed to the Son. Therefore, Jesus had *faith* like his Father to perform miracles.

From these documented statements, we know that Jesus "was guided from on high in a way that none other has ever been."[115] Truly, our Lord is "the replica of his Father—thinking, saying, *doing*, achieving, attaining, *as the Father has done before*."[116]

10

THE FATHER INTRODUCES HIS BELOVED SON—
A GRAND COUNCIL IN HEAVEN

By means of the Urim and Thummim, Abraham saw the great cosmic system that exists under the government of a great planet called Kolob. This governing orb is nearest to the residence of God, and Kolob controls all the planets belonging to the same universe as our earth (Abraham 3:1-10). In part of this great vision, Abraham saw "the intelligences that were organized before the world was" (Abraham 3:22). Elder McConkie says that "Abraham used the name *intelligences* to *apply to the spirit children of the Eternal Father."* [117]

According to the Prophet Joseph Smith, God the Father, who is "the head of the Gods called a council of the Gods; and they came together and" presented "a plan to create the world and people it" (*Teachings of the Prophet Joseph Smith*, p. 349).

At a solemn meeting, called the "Grand Council of heaven," the Father designated certain individuals who were to minister to the inhabitants of our world. These individuals were formally ordained to their various callings (*Teachings of the Prophet Joseph Smith*, p. 365).

THE ETERNAL FATHER AND HIS SON

God the Father formally introduced his plan of salvation to all of his spirit children. By laws not revealed, billions of spirit children were able to hear their Father speak.

As Elder McConkie has written:

> It was then explained that his spirit children would go down to earth, gain bodies of flesh and blood, be tried and tested in all things, and have opportunity by obedience to come back again to the Eternal Presence. It was then explained that one of the spirit children of the Father would be chosen to be the Redeemer and work out the infinite and eternal atonement. And it was then that the Father sent forth the call which said in substance and effect: Whom shall I send to be my Son in mortality? [118] (See Abraham 3:27).

From Abraham's record, we know that two mighty spirits answered the call. "One among them that was like unto God," who was Jesus Christ, said: "Here am I, send me" (Abraham 3:24, 27).

"And another," who was Lucifer, having authority in the presence of God (D&C 76:25-27), said, "Here am I, send me" (Abraham 3:27).

From the writings of Moses, we are given additional information concerning these two mighty spirits volunteering to be the Redeemer. Concerning the second volunteer, we learn that "Satan" wanted to amend the Father's eternal plan of salvation, and he said: "Behold, here am I, send me, I will be thy son, and I will redeem all mankind, that one soul shall not be lost, and surely I will do it; wherefore give me thine honor" (Moses 4:1).

Regarding the first volunteer, we read: "But, behold, *my Beloved Son*, which was my *Beloved* and *Chosen* from the beginning, said unto me—Father, thy will be done, and the glory be thine forever" (Moses 4:2). Here, we are informed that this first volunteer was "chosen," or foreordained, from the beginning by the Father to be the Redeemer.

Moses was then revealed the following: "Wherefore, because that Satan rebelled against me [and my plan of salvation, which plan has existed for eternity], and sought to destroy the agency of man, which I, the Lord God, had given him, and also, that I should give unto him mine own power . . . I caused that he should be cast down" (Moses 4:3).

With all of his spirit children in the "Grand Council" listening, the Father said of the two volunteers, *"I will send the first."* (Abraham 3: 27) (Italics added) Therefore, by combining the writings of Abraham and Moses, our Heavenly Father proclaimed to all of his spirit children, in the council, in substance and effect: *"I will send the first," "my Beloved Son"* (Jesus Christ), because he was "chosen from the beginning," to be the Redeemer (Moses 4:2; Abraham 3:24, 27).

AT THE BAPTISM OF GOD'S SON

As has been written previously in chapter two of this work, Jesus, who then was the mortal Son of God, came from Galilee to a river named Jordan to be baptized of John. After Jesus was totally immersed in water by John, we are informed that when Jesus came out of the water, the Spirit of God, which is the Holy Ghost, was seen descending from heaven to be with our Lord. Then, all who were present at this significant baptism, heard an audible voice from heaven saying, *"This is my beloved Son, in whom I am well pleased"* (Matthew 3: 13-17; compare Mark 1:9-11; Luke 3:21-22).

Concerning our Lord's baptism, Elder James E. Talmage says: "Jesus Christ thus humbly *complied with the will of the Father*, and was baptized by John by immersion in water. That his baptism was accepted as a pleasing and necessary act of submission was attested by what immediately ensued . . ." [119]

THE ETERNAL FATHER AND HIS SON

Then, Elder Talmage provides this interesting insight: "*Matthew records the Father's acknowledgment as given in the third person*, 'This is my beloved Son'; while both *Mark and Luke give the more direct address*, 'Thou art my beloved Son.' The variation, slight and essentially unimportant as it is though bearing on so momentous a subject, affords evidence of independent authorship and discredits any insinuation of collusion among the writers."[120]

From the Joseph Smith Translation of Matthew, this added information is given: "And lo, *he heard* [John] a voice from heaven, saying, This is my beloved Son, in whom I am well pleased. *Hear ye him*" (JST Matt. 3:46). Thus, the Father formally proclaimed his "beloved Son" and then declared, "Hear ye him." From this information, we are safe to believe that Jesus spoke and gave inspired teachings.

From the Joseph Smith Translation of Mark, we read: "And there came a voice from heaven, saying, Thou art my beloved Son, in whom I am well pleased. *And John bare record of it*" (JST Mark 1:9).

Concerning the baptism of our Lord, Elder McConkie has written:

". . . then John, and apparently also the whole assembled multitude, *heard the voice of the Father certify to Jesus' divine Sonship*. This was the Master's formal introduction to the world, *and in all solemnity and majesty the Father then and there decreed: "Hear ye him."*[121]

In another of his works, Elder McConkie wrote these words: "John sees the heavens open and the Holy Ghost descend in bodily form, in serenity and peace, like a dove. The sign of the dove is given, *and the voice of the Father*—graciously pleased that his Son has been baptized—*speaks*, and is heard by John's spiritually tuned ears and by the ears of all present who are in tune. It says: *"This is my beloved Son, in whom I am well pleased. Hear ye him."*

Repeating, our apostolic scholar writes: *"Hear Ye him!" The Father testifies of the Son; he introduces him to the world; and he commands: "Hear ye him!"* [122]

AT THE TRANSFIGURATION OF GOD'S SON

When Peter made his great confession that Jesus was the Christ, *the Son of the living God,* our Lord promised to give him the keys of the kingdom (Matt. 16:13-20; Mark 8:27-30; Luke 9:18-21). One week had elapsed between the day of promise and that glorious day when the keys were actually conferred upon the three presiding apostles (Matt. 17:1; Mark 9:2; Luke 9:28-36). The Joseph Smith Translation of Mark says, "Jesus taketh Peter, and James, and John, who asked him many questions concerning his sayings; and Jesus leadeth them up into a high mountain apart by themselves" (JST Mark 9:1). Luke informs us that Jesus took these three "up into a mountain to pray" (JST Luke 9:28). Most religious scholars believe that this "high mountain" was Mt. Hermon. [123]

From their climb up the mountain, and the late hour of the night, it was natural for Peter, James, and John to be tired; accordingly, these three "were heavy with sleep" (Luke 9: 32). While they were sleeping, Jesus went a short distance from them and prayed. Luke's record says: "And as he prayed, the fashion of his countenance was altered, and his raiment was white and glistering. And, behold, there talked with him two men, which were Moses and Elias: Who appeared in glory, and spake of his decease which he should accomplish at Jerusalem" (Luke 9:28-31).

The three presiding apostles were fully awakened from their deep sleep by "the surpassing splendor of the scene, and gazed with reverent awe upon their glorified Lord." [124] Matthew and Mark tell that Jesus "was transfigured" before Peter, James, and John (Matt.17:2; Mark 9:2).

THE ETERNAL FATHER AND HIS SON

From the Prophet Joseph Smith, we are given additional information of what happened on the mountain: "The Priesthood is everlasting. The Savior, Moses, and Elias, gave the keys to Peter, James, and John on the mount, *when they were transfigured before him*." [125] (italics added). In addition, these presiding apostles were able to see the future transfiguration of the earth (D&C 63:20-21).

Both Moses and Elias—who was Elijah—were speaking with Jesus. These ancient prophets were translated beings who had been taken into heaven without tasting death. By the laying on of hands with Jesus, Moses restored the keys of the gathering of Israel and of leading the Ten Tribes from the land of the north. Elijah restored the keys of the sealing power in order that whatever Peter, James, and John bound or loosed on earth would be bound or loosed in heaven. [126]

Not only did Moses and Elijah appear, but also John the Baptist, who was beheaded by the order of Herod the king (JST Mark 9:3). It may be that other unnamed prophets also appeared upon the Mount of Transfiguration.

Luke says, "While he [Peter] thus spake, there came a cloud, and overshadowed them: and they feared as they entered the cloud . . ." (Luke 9:34-35).

Matthew wrote: "While he [Jesus] yet spake, behold, a bright cloud overshadowed them . . ." (Matt. 17:5).

Concerning this cloud, Elder McConkie has written: "Not a watery cloud, but what the Jews called the *Shekinah* or *Dwelling Cloud*, the cloud which *manifested the presence and glory of God*. This cloud had rested upon the tabernacle in the wilderness (Num. 9:15-22), had covered Jehovah when he visited his people (Ex. 33:9-11; Num. 11:25), and is the one which enveloped Jesus, after his resurrection, when he *ascended to his Father*" (Acts 1:9).[127]

It was Elohim, the Eternal Father, who then spoke these familiar words: *"This is my beloved Son, in whom I am well pleased; hear ye him."* At the sound of that voice of Supreme Majesty, Peter, James, and John "were sore afraid" and fell to the ground (Matt. 17:6; JST Matt. 17:5).

Elder McConkie says: "Thus, once again the Divine Voice—the Father of us all . . . affirmed the eternal truth that Christ is the Son; that salvation comes by the Son; that all men must honor the Son and believe his words; that the only approved course for all men of all races in all ages is: "Hear ye him!" [128]

THE APPEARANCE OF GOD'S SON TO THE NEPHITES

One of the most inspiring events written in the Book of Mormon is the appearance of God's resurrected Son to about 2,500 men, women, and children, in the land Bountiful, as recorded in Third Nephi. Many members of the Church have concluded that our resurrected Lord appeared to the Nephite multitude following the three days of destruction and darkness upon the land. To help clarify when this dramatic event took place, we reply upon the knowledge of Dr. Sidney B. Sperry, a recognized LDS scholar:

> In verse 18 of chapter 10, Mormon anticipated the appearance of the resurrected Christ to his people, by pointing to the fact that He came apparently at the 'ending of the thirty-fourth year.' A comparison of this verse with 8:5 will show that nearly a year passed by after the great three days of darkness and destruction before our Lord appeared to the Nephites. This conclusion is borne out by a careful study of other facts in the record as written by Mormon." [129] In a footnote, he wrote this explanation: "Notice, for example, that at the end of the first day's ministry (19: 1-3) of the Savior to the Nephites, the people go casually to their homes and even know where to find their friends. This settled condition could scarcely have existed

immediately following the great destruction at the time of the Savior's death." [130]

In harmony with Dr. Sperry's comments regarding the time of the appearance of the resurrected Lord, Elder McConkie says: "The Nephites adjusted their calendar so as to begin a new dating era with the birth of Jesus; and according to their chronology, the storms and the darkness and the crucifixion came to pass on the fourth day of the first month of the thirty-fourth year (3 Ne. 8). Then 'in the ending' of that year (3 Ne. 10:18-19), several months after the Ascension on Olivet [in Jerusalem], Jesus ministered personally among the Nephites for many hours on many days." [131]

As the Nephite multitude were "conversing about this Jesus Christ, of whom the sign had been given concerning his death" they heard *"a voice as if it came out of heaven."* Their frames quaked, and their hearts burned as the *"small voice"* pierced them to the soul. They also heard the *voice a second time* without understanding it. The *third time*, they understood *"the voice which they heard"* that said: *"Behold my Beloved Son, in whom I am well pleased, in whom I have glorified my name—hear ye him"* (3 Ne. 11:1-7).

Once again the Divine Voice, the voice of the Father of us all, spoke to the Nephite multitude and introduced his Beloved Son and told the congregation: "Hear ye him." From Mormon's record, we are informed that the Father's voice was not "harsh," nor was it "loud," but it was a "small voice." Concerning this expression, the Prophet Joseph Smith revealed the following: "Yea, thus saith *the still small voice*, which whispereth through and pierceth all things, and often times it maketh my bones to quake while it maketh manifest . . ." (D&C 85:6) (Italics added) This likewise happened to the Nephite congregation. Finally hearing the "small voice" of the Father, *"it did pierce them that did hear to the center, insomuch that there was no part of their frame that it did not cause to quake; yea, it did pierce them to the very soul, and did cause their hearts to burn"* (3 Ne. 11:3) .This truly was a dynamic and choice experience for these blessed Nephite people to hear and feel the Father's voice introducing his Beloved Son.

THE FATHER INTRODUCES HIS SON TO JOSEPH SMITH, JR.

It is important to understand that the Dispensation of the Fulness of Times was to commence in the year 1820 and everything connected with this glorious event had to be in place. Joseph Smith, Jr. must be living in a home near Palmyra, New York. The Smith family must be religious, as well as lovingly supportive of each member of that household. An unusual excitement on the subject of religion must be in motion in that region. Young Joseph must read a passage from James, in the *Bible*, which would arouse a great desire in him to ask of God for an answer. Likewise, a grove of trees must be close to the Smith home so that God the Father and His Son could appear in privacy to the great Seer of the latter-days. Truly, Omnipotent Wisdom had left nothing to chance in these matters. Therefore, the hand of the Lord had planned and prepared all of those things in advance.

The foundation of The Church of Jesus Christ of Latter-day Saints is the First Vision. Of all the mysteries of the gospel, this one has caused countless numbers of people to either decry it or testify of its truthfulness. Accordingly, it is the greatest truth or the greatest fraud. As such, the Prophet's narrative says: "After I had retired to the place where I had previously designed to go, having looked around me, I kneeled down and began to offer up the desires of my heart to God" ("Joseph Smith—History" 1: 15).

As has been written, a grove of trees must be close to the Smith home so that God the Father and his Son could appear in privacy to the great Seer of the latter-days. With agency in full

THE ETERNAL FATHER AND HIS SON

force, we may properly believe that being spiritually attuned, Joseph was inspired to select the woods near his family home to ask of God. Accordingly, the grove of trees nearby became the "place where [he] had previously designed to go" ("Joseph Smith—History" 1:15).

While in the woods, it is worth noting that Joseph "looked around" to see if he was alone. Whether this looking was a natural reaction, or he sensed that some unseen person was watching him, we are not informed. Having satisfied himself that he was alone, he "kneeled down and began to offer up the desires of [his] heart to God." This young lad says, "I had scarcely done so, when immediately I was seized upon by some power which overcame me, and had such and astonishing influence over me as to bind my tongue so that I could not speak. Thick darkness gathered around me, and it seemed to me for a time as if I were doomed to sudden destruction" ("Joseph Smith—History" 1:15).

The Prophet says: "... just at this moment of great alarm, *I saw a pillar of light exactly over my head, above the brightness of the sun*, which descended gradually until it fell upon me.

"It no sooner appeared than I found myself delivered from the enemy which held me bound. When the light rested upon me I saw two Personages, whose brightness and glory defy all description, standing above me in the air. One of them spake unto me, calling me by name and said, pointing to the other—*This is my Beloved Son. Hear Him!*" ("Joseph Smith—History" 1:16-17).

To more fully understand the significance of this vision, we turn to the writings of Elder George Q. Cannon:

"... the deep gloom was rolled away and he saw a brilliant light. A pillar of celestial fire, far more glorious than the brightness of the noon-day sun, appeared directly above him. The defeated power fled with the darkness; and Joseph's spirit was free to worship and marvel at his deliverance. Gradually the light descended until it rested upon him; and he saw, standing above him in the air, enveloped in the pure radiance of the fiery pillar, two personages of incomparable beauty, alike in form and feature, and clad alike in snowy raiment. Sublime, dazzling, they filled his soul with awe. At length, One, calling Joseph by name, stretched His shining arm towards the Other, and said: *'This is my beloved son: hear him!'"* [132]

Concerning the Father's statement to the boy-prophet, Elder McConkie has penned these stirring words:

"Have more blessed words ever saluted human ears? Is it not again as it was at Bethabara when John Baptized the Lamb of God who takes away the sin of the world? Is it not once more as it was when the Son of God was transfigured before the chief of his ancient apostles?" [And we add: Is it not again when the resurrected Lord appeared to the Nephite multitude?] *The voice of God is heard again! The Father bears witness of the Son and introduces him to the world!"* [133]

As was written in Chapter 2, Elder Joseph Fielding Smith wrote this truth-filled statement:

"All revelation since the fall [of Adam] has come through Jesus Christ, who is the Jehovah of the Old Testament. In all of the scriptures, where God is mentioned and where he has appeared, it was Jehovah who talked with Abraham, with Noah, Enoch, Moses and all the prophets . . . *The Father has never dealt with man directly and personally since the fall, and he has never appeared except to introduce and bear record of the Son.* Thus the *Inspired Version* [which is now called the Joseph Smith Translation] records that *'no man hath seen God at any time, except he hath borne record of the Son . . .'"* (JST John 1: 19). [134]

From the four recorded instances where the Father proclaimed his Son, he only appeared, as far is recorded, to the

THE ETERNAL FATHER AND HIS SON

Joseph Smith, Jr., in the placed designated as the Sacred Grove. Here, the boy-prophet literally saw the Father and the Son, and consistently, the Father bore record of his Beloved Son, and let his Son give instruction and counsel to the boy-prophet.

Therefore, we humbly and gratefully announce that God the Father has in these last days restored the fulness of his everlasting gospel, for the salvation of mankind, by his Son. As Joseph Smith, Jr. says, this is how it happened: "One of them [God the *Eternal Father*] spake unto me, calling me by name and said, pointing to the other [Jesus Christ]—*This is My Beloved Son. Hear Him!*" ("Joseph Smith—History" 1:17).

11

JESUS TAUGHT HIS FATHER'S DOCTRINE—
"MY DOCTRINE IS NOT MINE"

During his later Judean ministry, Jesus attended and spoke at a festive Jewish celebration. "As originally established," says Elder James E. Talmage, "the Feast of Tabernacles was a seven day festival, followed by a holy convocation [assembly] on the eighth day. Each day was marked by special and in some respects distinctive services, all characterized by ceremonies of thanksgiving and praise." [135]

Our Lord did not come at the beginning of this celebration, but as John says, it was "about the midst of the feast"—perhaps about the fourth or fifth day—"Jesus went up into the temple, and taught" (John 7:14).

The fame of Jesus had spread like wildfire. The Galileans who preceded him to the celebration had told of the many miracles he had performed. His previous sermons and teachings, in other cities, had aroused great curiosity, as well as a diversity of opinion among the people.

John's record says: "And there was much murmuring among the people concerning him: for some said, He is a good man:

others said, Nay; but he deceiveth the people" (John 7:12).

It seems that all who were at this celebration were seeking our Lord, for the people asked with great anticipation, "Where is he?" (John 7:11). The multitude wanted to know if the reports of him were true; is he was the promised Messiah; is he the person who will deliver us from Roman bondage; and is he really the Son of God?

Concerning what happened that day, John only informs us that our Lord came into the temple and "taught" (John 7:14). The scriptural record does not inform of us of what he said. "Based on the responses that were forthcoming," says Elder Bruce R. McConkie, ". . . there is little doubt as to the substance and purport of what he then said . . . *Jesus preached the gospel*. This gospel is that he came into the world to work out the infinite and eternal atonement; that he is God's Son, the Promised Messiah; and that if men [and women] will believe in him and live his law they will be raised not alone in immortality but unto everlasting life in the Everlasting Presence." [136]

As explained in Chapter 3, then bishop Orson F. Whitney expressed these inspired teachings: "There is but one way, one plan of life and salvation, and there need be but one; for God, being an economist, does not create that which is superfluous; and there can be, in the very nature of things, only one true plan of eternal life . . . Thus it is that the Latter-day Saints preach the everlasting gospel, the unchangeable way of eternal life." [137] In the temple that day at the Feast of Tabernacles, Jesus *taught* the people his Father's gospel—the only true plan of life and salvation (John 7:14).

Because of these teachings by Jesus at the Feast of Tabernacles, "the Jews marvelled," and they asked, "How knoweth this man letters, having never learned?" (John 7:15).

Regarding this question asked by the Jewish teachers, Elder Talmage explains: "He was no graduate of their schools; He had never sat at the feet of their rabbis; He had not been officially accredited by them nor licensed to teach. Whence came His wisdom, before which all their academic attainments were as nothing? Jesus answered their troubled queries, saying: *'My doctrine is not mine, but his that sent me.'* 'If any man will do his will, he shall know of the doctrine, whether it be of God, or whether I speak of myself'" (See John 7:16-17).[138]

Then, this explanatory comment is given by our apostolic scholar: "His [Jesus'] Teacher, greater even than Himself, was the *Eternal Father*, whose will he proclaimed . . . The Master proceeded to show that a man who speaks on his own authority alone seeks to aggrandize himself. Jesus did not so; *He honored His Teacher, His Father, His God, not Himself . . .*" [139] (See John 7:18).

In reference to our Lord's comment, "My doctrine is not mine, but his that sent me," Elder McConkie gives these thoughts: *"The Father, not the Son, is the Author of the plan of salvation. This plan embodies the Father's doctrine, the Father's laws, the Father's gospel.* He ordained and announced the whole plan of creation, redemption, salvation, and exaltation, and he chose one of his spirit offspring to be born into the world as his Son to work out the infinite and eternal atonement—all in accordance with his will. *The laws which must be obeyed to gain salvation are spoken of as the gospel of Jesus Christ* because our Lord himself conformed to them perfectly, adopted them as his own, *taught them in the power of his Father*, and worked out the atoning sacrifice, by means of which they gained full force and validity." [140]

As has been explained in the previous chapter, the Father introduced his Son in mortality on four recorded instances, and told those who were there on those sacred occasions: "Hear Him!" It was the Son, not the Father, who gave instruction and teachings. Why? In all respects, the Son of God is like his Father. They think alike; they speak the same eternal truths; and every action taken by the one is the same thing the other would do

THE ETERNAL FATHER AND HIS SON

under the same circumstances (John 12: 44-45; 14: 6-20). As such, Jesus answered the Jews at the Feast of Tabernacles, "My doctrine is not mine, but his [my Father] that sent me" (John 7:16).

JESUS TAUGHT THE GOSPEL OF THE KINGDOM

Matthew's gospel tells that after Jesus was tempted of the devil in the wilderness, and after he heard that John, who baptized him, was cast into prison, "he departed into Galilee" (Matthew 4:12). Then, this significant statement is written: "From that time Jesus began to preach, and say, *Repent: for the kingdom of heaven is at hand"* (Matthew 4:17). It is worth pointing out that previous to this time, the man who baptized Jesus preached the identical message: "In those days came John the Baptist, preaching in the wilderness of Judea. And saying, *Repent ye: for the kingdom of heaven is at hand"* (Matthew 3: 1-2, italics added). Why? It is the same eternal gospel message. A man must repent of his sins and be baptized for the remission of sins (3 Ne. 27: 20). No unclean thing can enter into the kingdom of heaven (1 Ne. 10:21; Moses 6:57). Even though our Lord was sinless, he was baptized to fulfill all righteousness (Matt. 3:15). Therefore, God's Son set the perfect example for all of us.

Giving further information, Mark says: "Now after that John was put in prison, Jesus came into Galilee, preaching the gospel of the kingdom of God, And saying, "The time is fulfilled [of the prophecies of the Promised Messiah], and the kingdom of God is at hand: repent ye, and believe the gospel" (Mark 1:14-15).

Luke also tells what happened in Galilee: "And Jesus returned in the power of the Spirit into Galilee: and there went out a fame of him through all the region round about. And he taught in their synagogues . . ." (Luke 4: 14-15).

Lastly, John says: Now after two days he departed thence, and went into Galilee. For Jesus himself testified, that a prophet hath no honour in his own country . . . So Jesus came again into Cana of Galilee, where he made the water wine . . ." (John 4:43-46).

From these writings, we are informed that from the time that Jesus began his formal ministry in Galilee, he told the people to repent of their sins and believe the gospel. Later in his ministry, our Lord said, *"I am the Son of God"* (John 10:36, italics added). He taught that mankind must believe in him as the promised Messiah; that they must repent of their sins, and be baptized by immersion in water by a legal administrator, receive the gift of the Holy Ghost by the laying on of hands, and then endure in righteousness to the end of their mortal life. Elder McConkie has written: "He taught that the gospel or plan of salvation was being restored in his day, so that if men [and women] would believe and obey, they could gain peace in this life and eternal life in the world to come. He taught exactly, precisely, and identically what he has told the elders of Israel to teach in this day." [141]

It is noteworthy that in Galilee our Lord began his formal ministry, as well as performed his first known miracle, turning water into wine, at a marriage in "Cana of Galilee" (John 2:11).[142]

From the writings of Matthew, Mark, Luke, and John, we are plainly told that Jesus preached the gospel. The gospel taught by God's Son is the Father's gospel; it is the Father's eternal plan of salvation; and it is the only true plan of eternal life.

DID JESUS TEACH: "GOD IS A SPIRIT"?

While speaking to "a woman of Samaria," Jesus said: "But the hour cometh, and now is, when the true worshippers *shall worship the Father in spirit and in truth: For the Father seeketh such to worship him"* (John 4:23, italics added). Then,

THE ETERNAL FATHER AND HIS SON

as it is recorded in the King James Version of the Bible, our Lord said: *"God is a Spirit:* and they that worship *him* must worship him in spirit and in truth." (John 4:7,24, italics added).

This singular statement, supposedly spoken by God's Son, has caused many in the sectarian world to believe that the Father is literally a Spirit. From the Joseph Smith Translation of John, we are informed of what Jesus actually told this woman: *"For unto such hath God promised his Spirit. And they who worship him, must worship in spirit and in truth"* (JST John 4:26).

Based on this information, Elder McConkie has written these words: *"What marvels of mischief one mistranslated phrase has done!* Jesus never, never, never said, 'God is a Spirit,' but rather that God had promised his Spirit unto those who worship him in Spirit and in truth.* Yet, falsely supposing our Lord to be the author of this statement, the whole sectarian world has turned to it, more than to any other single passage, to find support for their false creeds." [143]

From inspired teachings given by the Prophet Joseph Smith, the Latter-days Saint people know this correct doctrine: "The Father has a body of flesh and bones as tangible as man's; the Son also . . . but the Holy Ghost has not a body of flesh and bones, but is a personage of Spirit" (D&C 130:22). Thus, he is a Spirit man. Based on this knowledge, we continue again with Elder McConkie's words: "There is a sense in which it might be said, without impropriety, that God [the Father] is a Spirit . . . when it is remembered that a spirit is a personage, an entity, a living personality whose body is made of more pure and refined substance than the temporal bodies of men [and women] . . . then it might truly be said that God is a spirit. He is a Spirit Personage, a Personage with a body of flesh and bones . . . He is a Spirit in the same sense that all men are spirits, and in the sense that all men [and women] eventually will have resurrected or spiritual bodies as contrasted with their present natural or mortal bodies" (1 Cor. 15:42-50; D&C 88:25-28). [144]

Therefore, Jesus correctly taught the "woman of Samaria" the Father's doctrine. This doctrine was not that God the Father was a Spirit, but those who worship him in spirit and in truth, God hath "promised his Spirit" (JST John 4:26).

JESUS TEACHES HIS RELATIONSHIP TO THE FATHER

Near the end of his mortal ministry, Jesus was in Jerusalem at the temple. While there, he publicly uttered a solemn testimony of his divinity. With a loud voice, he said to the priestly rulers and the multitude in general: "He that believeth on me, believeth not on me, *but on him that sent me*" (John 12:44, italics added). Then, he spoke this revealing doctrine: "And he that seeth me seeth him that sent me" (John 12:45).

These teachings emphasized that those who believed he was the Son of God, must also believe in his Father who sent him. Here, Jesus is speaking plainly and openly to those people who were listening. The Son, in all respects, is like his Father. They think alike, they look alike; they speak the same eternal truths, preach the same gospel, and every action taken by the one is the same thing the other would do under the same circumstances (John 12:44-45; 14:6-20).

The gospel message our Lord preached during his mortal ministry would be a means of judgment and condemnation to all who willfully rejected it. (See John 12:48). By way of solemn testimony, Jesus said: "For I have not spoken of myself; but the Father which sent me, he gave me a commandment, what I should say, and what I should speak. And I know that his commandment is life everlasting: *whatsoever I speak therefore, even as the Father said unto me, so I speak*" (John 12:49-50).

Elder McConkie asks this question: "Who is this Son of Man?" Answering, he writes: "He is the Son of God who speaks the word of the Father, and the Father's commandments lead men to eternal life, which is the greatest of all the gifts of God.

"Thus Jesus ended his public teaching: ended it with a testimony of his own divine Sonship; ended it with a call to all men to believe in him and live his laws; ended it with the promise that all the obedient shall have eternal life in his Father's kingdom.

"With this he left the temple forever." [145]

From these teachings spoken by our Lord in Jerusalem, we know that Jesus only taught his Father's gospel. As has been explained previously in this chapter, the Father is author of the plan of salvation. This plan embodies the Father's doctrine and laws. Our Lord conformed to those doctrines and laws perfectly, and he adopted them as his own. Jesus taught the Father's gospel so that others might have an opportunity to have eternal life. By obedience to the teachings of the gospel, which is the eternal plan of salvation, we can become like the Eternal Father.

12

WHO HAS SEEN GOD THE FATHER?—
ADAM AND EVE

Adam and his wife, Eve, walked and talked with their Father. (Gen. 1; 3; Abraham 5; Moses 3; 4; 5; 6:22; Chapter 6). Concerning this glorious association, Elder McConkie says:

> Adam . . . was the first of the earth's inhabitants to see the Lord. *He and his wife, Eve, had intimate and extended association with both the Father and the Son before the fall and while they dwelt in Eden's hallowed vales* (Moses 3 and 4). *They then knew, before mortality entered the world, that they were the offspring of Exalted Parents in whose image they were made.* It was as automatic and instinctive for them to know their ancestry, their family relationship, and the exalted destiny they might obtain, as it is for mortal children to grow and assume they will be like their parents. [146]

We do not know how long Adam and Eve lived in the Garden of Eden and personally associated with their resurrected Father.

THE ETERNAL FATHER AND HIS SON

Whether their time in the Garden was long or short, Adam and Eve had the glorious privilege of personally seeing and conversing with their Father frequently.

After the fall, Adam and Eve were "cast out from the Garden of Eden" (Gen. 3:23-24; Moses 4:29, 31; D&C 29:40-41). Consequently, they were shut out from the presence of their Father and denied the privilege of personally seeing and speaking with him. Following the expulsion from Eden, Adam was visited by angels, *heard the voice of God*, received revelation and directions, and was in tune with the Spirit (D&C 29:41-42; Moses 5:4, 6; 6:22).

ENOCH

From the writings of Moses, we find that Enoch and the inhabitants of the holy city he built were the first people who were translated (Hebrew 11:5).[147] We further learn that Enoch was a spiritual giant. His faith was so great that when he spoke the word of the Lord, the "earth trembled, and the mountains fled," and the "rivers of water were turned out of their course," and "all nations feared greatly, so powerful was the word of Enoch, and so great was the power of the language which God had given him" (Moses 7:13).

After those in the city of Zion were translated and "taken up into heaven, Enoch beheld, and lo, all the nations of the earth were before him" (Moses 7:23; Hebrews 11:5). Then, "Enoch was ... lifted up *even in the bosom of the Father*, and of the Son of Man ..." (Moses 7:24). Concerning this statement, Elder McConkie says: " ... which is to say *that he saw both the Father* and the Son and conversed with them. There are then recorded some three and a half pages of these conversations, some statements being made by the Father, others by the Son."[148] This is the second recorded instance where a prophet of God saw God the Father, as well as his premortal Son. Enoch truly was a righteous man of God.

JOSEPH SMITH, JR.

As stated in Chapters 1 and 10, Joseph Smith, Jr., lad of 14, saw the Father and the Son. Joseph said: "It was on the morning of a beautiful, clear day, early in the spring of eighteen hundred and twenty" ("Joseph Smith—History" 1:14).

Why this particular day? This was the precise "day" designated by the Father and Son to usher in the final dispensation of the fulness of times. In addition, this appearance happened while Joseph was fully awake. Accordingly, no one can attribute this appearance to a dream that Joseph had during the night.

Telling what transpired in the "woods" that day, the boy-prophet testifies: "I saw a pillar of light exactly over my head, *above the brightness of the sun*, which descended gradually until it fell upon me" ("Joseph Smith—History" 1:14-16).

Continuing with the official version, Joseph says, "When the light rested upon me *I saw two Personages*, whose brightness and glory defy all description, standing above me in the air. One of them spake unto me, calling me by name and said, pointing to the other—This is my Beloved Son. Hear Him!" ("Joseph Smith—History" 1:17). It was God the Father introducing his Son to the boy Joseph.

Concluding his remarks concerning this glorious vision, Joseph simply says: "He again forbade me to join any [church]; and many other things did he say unto me, which I cannot write at this time." Then, he tells what happened to him when the vision ended: "When I came to myself again, I found myself lying on my back, looking up into heaven. When the Light departed, I had no strength; but soon recovering in some degree, I went home" ("Joseph Smith—History" 1: 19-20).

Regarding this marvelous vision, we conclude by using the words of the Lord's anointed: " . . . I had actually seen a light, and *in the midst of that Light I saw two Personages, and they did in reality speak to me*; and though I was hated

THE ETERNAL FATHER AND HIS SON

and persecuted for saying that I had seen a vision, *yet it was true*; I knew it, and I knew that God knew it, and I could not deny it, neither dared I do it; at least I knew that by so doing I would offend God, and come under condemnation" ("Joseph Smith—History" 1:25).

Thus, Adam, Enoch, and Joseph Smith, Jr. are three witnesses to the truth that they have seen God the Father. It is worth emphasizing that Adam saw the Father while he was immortal. Enoch saw the Father after he became a translated being.[149] Therefore, in 1820, Joseph Smith, Jr. was *the only mortal being*—a being with blood flowing in his veins—who saw the Father. Truly, the Prophet Joseph Smith ranks as one of the greatest prophets.

JOSEPH SMITH, JR. AND SIDNEY RIGDON

In one of the most remarkable visions given in mortality, the Vision of the Degrees of Glory, on February 16, 1832, the Prophet Joseph Smith and Sidney Rigdon saw both the Father and the Son. From their combined testimonies, we read: "And we beheld the glory of the Son, *on the right hand of the Father* . . . (D&C 76:20).

In this same vision, they further say: "For we saw him [Jesus Christ], *even on the right hand of God* . . ." (D&C 76:23)

Concerning this vision, Elder McConkie has written these words: "After Joseph Smith and Sidney Rigdon had *seen the Father* and the Son . . . their continued language says: 'Great and marvelous are the works of the Lord, and the mysteries of his kingdom which he showed unto us . . .'" (D&C 76:114-118). [150]

BRUCE E. DANA

AT THE NEWLY COMPLETED KIRTLAND TEMPLE

On January 21, 1836, the first meeting was held in the newly completed Kirtland Temple.[151] With others present, the Prophet Joseph Smith received the following vision:

"The heavens were opened upon us, and I beheld the celestial kingdom of God, and the glory thereof . . . Also the blazing throne of God, *whereon was seated the Father* and the Son . . ." (D&C 137:1-3).[152]

From what has been recorded, this is the third time that the Prophet Joseph Smith saw God the Father. The first time was in 1820; the second time was in 1832; and the third time was in 1836.

NEWEL KNIGHT

During the last week in May, 1830, Newel Knight came to Fayette, New York and was baptized by David Whitmer. On the ninth of June, 1830, the first Conference of the Church was held.[153] While at this Conference, Newel Knight saw heaven open and beheld the Lord Jesus Christ, *seated on the right hand of the Father.* Following this experience, Brother Knight rehearsed to the Prophet Joseph Smith the glorious things which he had seen and felt, while he was in the spirit.[154]

LYMAN WIGHT

At the Conference of the Church held June 3-6, 1831, the Spirit of the Lord came upon the Prophet Joseph Smith and he prophesied various things. Concluding his remarks, the Prophet laid his hands upon Lyman Wight and ordained him a High Priest. Following this ordination, the spirit of the Lord fell came upon Brother Wight and he prophesied concerning

THE ETERNAL FATHER AND HIS SON

the coming of Christ. At the conclusion of his remarks, Lyman saw the heavens open and the Son of Man *sitting on the right hand of the Father*, making intercession for his brethren, the Saints." [155]

JOSEPH SMITH, JR. AND ZEBEDEE COLTRIN

In 1883, "Brother Zebedee Coltrin said: I believe I am the only living man now in the church who was connected with the School of the Prophets when it was organized in 1833.[156] (See D&C 88:127; 90:7, 13).

"At *one of those meetings after* the organization of the school . . . on the 23 of January, 1833, *when we were all together*, [the Prophet] Joseph having given instructions, and while engaged in silent prayer . . . a personage walked through the room from East to West, and Joseph asked if we saw him. I [Zebedee] saw him and suppose the others did, and Joseph answered that is Jesus, the Son of God, our elder brother . . . *Another person came through*; *He was surrounded as with a flame of fire*. He (Zebedee) experienced a sensation that it might destroy the tabernacle as it was of consuming fire of great brightness. *The Prophet said this was the Father of our Lord Jesus Christ. I saw him.*"

When asked about the kind of clothing the Father has on, Brother Coltrin said:

> I did not discover His clothing for He was surrounded as with a flame of fire, which was so brilliant that I could not discover anything else but His person. I saw His hands, His legs, his feet, his eyes, nose, mouth, head and body in the shape and form of a perfect man. He sat in a chair as a man would sit in a chair, but this appearance was so grand and overwhelming that it seemed I should melt down in His presence, and the sensation was so powerful that it thrilled through my whole system and I

felt it in the marrow of my bones. The Prophet Joseph said: Brethren, now you are prepared to be the apostles of Jesus Christ [not ordained in the Quorum of the Twelve, but to be special witnesses], *for you have seen both the Father and the Son, and know that they exist and that they are two separate personages.*" [157]

ALFRED DOUGLAS YOUNG

An early convert of the Church was Alfred Douglas Young. While conversing with his brother on the morning of September 17, 1841, concerning the principles of the gospel, he was prompted by the Spirit to go to some secret place. He went to the woods near his brother's home, and an angel beckoned him in vision by saying, "Follow thou me."

Concerning this angelic personage, Brother Young says: "He ascended upward in the direction from whence he came and I followed him. *He took me into the presence of God the Father* and his Son Jesus Christ. There was a rail between us; but I saw them seated on a throne."

Later, he writes: "While I prayed the rail was removed and I stood upon my feet. Jesus arose and stepped from the side of his Father and came near where I stood. *I was in their presence and I gazed upon their glory. . .*" [158]

How many more have seen the Father in these Latter-days, we are left to wonder. We are thankful for those who have recorded their testimony of seeing God the Father.

13

WHO HAS SEEN GOD'S SON?— MANY SAW THE PREMORTAL LORD

As written in the previous chapter, Adam, Enoch, and Joseph Smith, Jr. have seen God's Son. Giving us further information, Elder McConkie has written these words: "We have in Holy Writ numerous accounts of prophets and holy men who have see the Lord—some face to face, others in dreams and visions; some in his glory, others when that glory was withheld from mortal view. These accounts have been preserved for us as examples and patterns of what has been, what is, and what yet shall be. . . ."[159]

Excepting with Adam and Enoch, the Eternal Father appears for the main purpose of introducing his Son. For as the original writing of John says, "And no man hath seen God [the Father] at any time, except he hath borne record of the Son . . ." (JST John 1:19). This is what is involved in the law of intercession and of mediation (Mosiah 15:8; 2 Ne. 2:9-10, 28). The Lord is the Mediator between God and man (JST 1 Tim. 2:4-6). Unless men and women accept the Son of God, they cannot receive the Father. Jesus declared, "No man cometh unto the Father, but by me" (John 14:6).

With this stated, we shall consider some of the important appearances of the premortal Lord to various mortals on this earth. We begin with appearances during the time of Adam.

SETH

"And Adam [the husband of Eve] lived one hundred and thirty years, and begat a son . . . and called his name Seth" (Gen. 4:25-26; 5:3; Moses 6:10; Luke 3:38). At the age of 69, this righteous son was ordained by Adam and given the priesthood (D&C 107:42; D&C 84:16). Seth is called "a perfect man, and his likeness was the express likeness of his father, insomuch that he seemed to be like unto his father in all things, and could be distinguished from him only by his age" (D&C 107:43). Three years previous to his death, Adam called *Seth*, and others, into the valley of Adam-ondi-Ahman, and while there, *"the [premortal] Lord appeared unto them"* (D&C 107:53). We know not what was said by the Lord to Seth and others. Someday, perhaps, this knowledge will be revealed.

MANY AT ADAM-ONDI-AHMAN

In addition to *Adam* and his son, *Seth*, the following individuals saw the premortal Lord at Adam-ondi-Ahman:
Enos—a son of Seth (Gen. 4:26; 5:6; Luke 3:38).
Cainan—a son of Enos (Gen. 5:9; Luke 3:37-38).
Mahalaleel—a son of Cainan (Gen. 5:12; Luke 3:37).
Jared—a son of Mahalaleel (Gen. 5:15; Luke 3:37).
Enoch—a son of Jared (Gen. 5:18: Luke 3:37).
Methuselah—a son of Enoch (Gen. 5:21; Luke 3:37).
As was written in the previous chapter, Enoch eventually became a translated being (Hebrews 11:5). After he was translated, he saw both the Father and the Son (Moses 7:24). The appearance of the premortal Lord at Adam-ondi-Ahman is

written in the "book of Enoch" (D&C 107:57). However, we only have a small portion of Enoch's prophecies and writings (Moses 6; 7; D&C 107:56-57).

The *"residue of [Adam's] posterity who were righteous,"* met at Adam-ondi-Ahman (D&C 107:53-54, italics added). We are not informed of how many of this righteous posterity saw the premortal Lord; however, we may safely believe that it involved a vast number of people. Truly these individuals were righteous. By their faith and obedience to the commandments of God, they were blessed to see the premortal Lord.

ABRAHAM

Originally Abraham's name was Abram (Gen. 11:26; 17:5). He was the son of Terah, and Abram was born in Ur of the Chaldees (Gen. 11:26-28). After his father died, Abram journeyed to Canaan. There in Haran, at Canaan, he received a divine call (Gen. 11:31; 12:1-4; 17). Later, his name was changed to Abraham (Gen. 17:5).

Abraham saw the premortal Lord several times because of his faith and righteousness. At a time that the Pharaoh's priests attempted to sacrifice Abraham upon an altar, this righteous man pleaded to the Lord for deliverance. At that moment, this great man says: "He filled me with the vision of the Almighty . . . And his voice was unto me: Abraham, Abraham, behold, my name is Jehovah, and I have heard thee and have come down to deliver thee . . ." (Abraham 1:15-16).

Because the Lord instructed him, Abraham "left the land of Ur, of the Chaldees, to go into the land of Canaan" (Abraham 2:4). Again in Haran, he says, "the Lord appeared unto me, and said unto me . . . For I am the Lord thy God; I dwell in heaven; the earth is my footstool . . . My name is Jehovah, and I know the end from the beginning; therefore my hand shall be over thee. And I will make of thee a great nation, and I will bless thee above measure, and make thy name great among all nations, and thou shalt be a blessing unto thy seed after thee, that in their hands they shall bear this ministry and Priesthood unto all nations" (Abraham 2:6-9).

At another appearance, his record says: "Thus I, Abraham, talked with the Lord, face to face, as one man talketh with another; and he told me of the works which his hands had made; And he said unto me: My son, my son (and his hand was stretched out), behold I will show you all these. And he put his hand upon mine eyes, and I saw those things which his hands had made, which were many; and they multiplied before mine eyes, and I could not see the end thereof" (Abraham 3:11-12).

In Genesis, as recorded in the King James Version of the Bible, there are other accounts of some of the appearances of the Lord to Abraham. While his name was Abram, "he passed through the land unto the place of Sichem, unto the plain of Moreh." While there, the record says, "And the Lord appeared unto Abram . . ." (Gen. 12:6-7).

After returning from Egypt, "Abram dwelled in the land of Canaan." Here, the record says, "And the Lord said unto Abram . . . Lift up now thine eyes . . . For all the land which thou seest, to thee will I give it, and to thy seed forever" (Gen. 13:12-15). It is implied that this was a personal visitation, but we are not specifically told.

In addition, the record says, "And when Abram was ninety years old and nine, the Lord appeared to Abram, and said unto him, I am the Almighty God; walk before me, and be thou perfect. And I will make my covenant between me and thee, and will multiply thee exceedingly" (Gen. 17:1-2).

Lastly, the record says: "And the Lord appeared unto him [Abram] in the plains of Mamre . . ." (Gen. 18:1).

Truly Abraham was a righteous prophet who was blessed many times to see the premortal Lord. It needs to be emphasized that these visitations were due to his great faith and obedience.

MOSES

One of the greatest prophets was Moses. He is known as the great law-giver of Israel. From the accounts written in the Old Testament and those from the Book of Moses, we are made aware of some of the great works of this ancient seer. The miracles attending his ministry have rarely been duplicated. As a translated being, he appeared on the mount of transfiguration and with our Lord restored keys upon Peter, James, and John (Matt. 17:1-3; Mark 9:2-4; Luke 9:28-32).[160]

Then, as a resurrected being, he appeared to the Prophet Joseph Smith and Oliver Cowdery in the Kirtland Temple and committed unto them keys of the gathering of Israel, and the leading of the ten tribes from the land of the north (D&C 110:11).

Aaron and Miriam complained against Moses, a man most meek of all men. With Moses present, the premortal Lord, while in a cloud, told Aaron and Miriam: "With him [Moses] will I speak mouth to mouth . . . and the similitude of the Lord shall he behold" (Numbers 12:1-8). This promise was verified by this statement: "And there arose not a prophet since in Israel like unto Moses, whom the Lord knew face to face" (Deut. 34:10).

Previous to this time, we read: "And the Lord spake unto Moses face to face, as a man speaketh unto his friend" (Ex. 33:11). Likewise, it is written: "And behold, the glory of the Lord was upon Moses, so that Moses stood in the presence of God, and talked with him face to face" (Moses 1:31).

Prior to Moses going into the mount to receive the tables of stone containing the commandments, the premortal Lord appeared to Moses and other men. "Then went up Moses, and Aaron, Nadab, and Abihu, and seventy of the elders of Israel: And they saw the God of Israel and there was under his feet as it were a paved work of sapphire stone . . ." (Ex. 24: 9-11).

Lastly, we are informed that "Moses was caught up into an exceedingly high mountain, and he saw God face to face, and he talked with him, and the glory of God was upon Moses; therefore Moses could endure his presence" (Moses 1:2).

After Moses had seen "the world and the ends thereof," and gained knowledge of many things, he revealed: "But now mine own eyes have beheld God; but not my natural, but my spiritual eyes, for my natural eyes could not have beheld; for I should have withered and died in his presence; but his glory was upon me; and I beheld his face, for I was transfigured before him" (Moses 1:11). Thus, these various accounts of the premortal Lord speaking face to face with Moses, verifies that Moses truly was a mighty prophet of God.

OTHER RIGHTEOUS INDIVIDUALS

To ***Isaac***, the son of Abraham and Sarah (Gen. 17:15-19), the premortal Lord "appeared unto him, and said, Go not down into Egypt; dwell in the land which I shall tell thee of" (Gen. 26:1-6).

Jacob, the younger of the twin sons of Isaac and Rebekah (Gen. 25: 20-26), had a special dream. In it, he saw a "ladder set up on the earth, and the top of it reached to heaven . . . And, behold, the Lord stood above it, and said, I am the Lord God of Abraham . . . and the God of Isaac: the land whereon thou liest, to thee will I give it, and to thy seed" (Gen. 28:12-13).

Jacob also says, "I have seen God face to face, and my life is preserved" (Gen. 32:30). Lastly, we are informed that "God appeared unto Jacob again, when he came out of Padanaram, and blessed him. And God said unto him, Thy name is Jacob: thy name shall not be called any more Jacob, *but Israel shall be thy name* . . ." (Gen. 35: 9-10).

Joshua: We are informed that "after the death of Moses . . . it came to pass, that the Lord spake unto Joshua the son of Nun, Moses' minister," saying, "Moses my servant is dead; now therefore arise, go over this Jordan [river], thou, and all this

THE ETERNAL FATHER AND HIS SON

people, unto the land which I do give to them, even to the children of Israel" (Joshua 1:1-2). It is implied that the Lord appeared and spoke to Joshua, but we are not fully informed.

Solomon: We are informed that "Solomon loved the Lord, walking in the statutes of [king] David his father . . ." (1 Kings 3:3). In a place called Gibeon, "the Lord appeared to Solomon in a dream by night; and God said, Ask what I shall give thee" (1 Kings 3:5).

Again, we read: "And it came to pass, when Solomon had finished the building of the house of the Lord . . . the Lord appeared to Solomon the second time, as he had appeared unto him at Gibeon" (1 Kings 9:1-2).

Though Solomon was righteous during most of his life, we sadly read these words: "For it came to pass, when Solomon was old, that his wives turned away his heart after other gods: and his heart was not perfect with the Lord his God . . . And the Lord was angry with Solomon, because his heart was turned away from the Lord God of Israel, *which had appeared unto him twice*" (1 Kings 11:4, 9).

This demonstrates that though a person is highly blessed to see the Lord, that individual must remain faithful to the end. Solomon willfully turned away from the Lord, and followed idle gods. As such, he lost favor with the Lord.

Isaiah: A mighty prophet for forty years in Jerusalem. Isaiah is one of the most quoted of all the prophets. This great man is quoted by Jesus, Paul, Peter, and John. In addition, Isaiah is quoted in the Book of Mormon and the Doctrine and Covenants.

From the writings of Isaiah, in the Bible, we read: "In the year that king Uzziah died I saw also the Lord sitting upon a throne, high and lifted up, and his train filled the temple" (Isaiah 6:1-5).

Ezekiel: At the beginning of the book of Ezekiel, he says that he was a priest (Ezekiel 1:3). For 22 years, he gave various prophecies. Ezekiel received many visions, and spoke much about the restoration of Israel. In addition, he spoke of the millennial reign of the Lord. Latter-day revelation confirms the authenticity of his writings (D&C 29:21).

Ezekiel says: "The heavens were opened, and I saw visions of God" (Ezekiel 1:1). Likewise, he was able to see the throne and the glory of God (Ezekiel 10). It is implied that he saw God, but we are not fully informed.

Daniel: Was a righteous youth. We read that he and three of his companions refused to eat the rich food of king Nebuchadnezzar (Daniel 1). Daniel also interpreted the king's dream, in which the kingdom of God in the last days is depicted (Daniel 2). Because of his faith and righteousness, Daniel saw the Lord and others in a glorious vision (Chapter 10).

From what is written in the Old Testament of the Bible, the above mentioned individuals saw the premortal Lord. All of this was due to their faith and righteousness. We now turn our attention to one of the greatest appearances of the premortal Lord, as recorded in the Book of Mormon.

THE BROTHER OF JARED AND OTHERS

One of the most inspiring events written in the Book of Mormon is the appearance of the premortal Lord to the brother of Jared on "mount Shelem" (Either 3:1). From what was revealed to the Prophet Joseph Smith, we are given the name of Jared's brother—Mahonri Moriancumer. [161] It is worth noting that the place on the shore of the great sea where Jared and his people dwelt for four years before crossing to America is called "Moriancumer" (Ether 2:13).

Approximately 1750 years elapsed from Adam's dispensation to the ministry of Mahonri. From Moroni's abridgement of the Book of Ether, we are informed that the brother of Jared took "sixteen small stones," which "were white and clear, even as

THE ETERNAL FATHER AND HIS SON

transparent glass; and he did carry them in his hands upon the top of the mount." There, he prayed in mighty faith, saying: "O Lord . . . touch these stones . . . with thy finger, and prepare them that they may shine forth in darkness; and they shall shine forth unto us in the vessels which we have prepared, that we may have light while we shall cross the sea" (Ether 3:1-4).

The record goes on to say: "And it came to pass that when the brother of Jared had said these words, behold, the Lord stretched forth his hand and touched the stones one by one with his finger." So great was Mahonri's faith the "veil was taken from off the eyes of the brother of Jared, and he saw the finger of the Lord, and it was as the finger of a man, *like unto flesh and blood*" (Ether 3:6). This statement written by Moroni gives support to the belief that spirit personages have color or pigmentation, the same as mortals do. In support of this statement, we continue with the conversation between the premortal Lord and Mahonri. After the brother of Jared fell down to the ground because "he was struck with fear," the Lord said and asked him: "Arise, why hast thou fallen?" (Ether 3:7).

Mahonri answered: "I saw the finger of the Lord . . . *for I knew not that the Lord had flesh and blood*" (Ether 3:8).

The Lord responded: "Because of thy faith thou hast seen that I shall take upon me flesh and blood." Continuing, our Lord declared: "Never has man come before me with such exceeding faith as thou hast; for were it not so ye could not have seen my finger." Then, this interesting question is asked of Mahonri: "Sawest thou more than this?" (Ether 3:9).

He answered: "Nay; Lord." Then, boldly Mahonri asked: "Show thyself unto me" (Ether 3:9).

The Lord then "showed himself unto him, and said: Because thou knowest these things ye are redeemed from the fall [of Adam] . . . Behold, I am he who was prepared from the foundation of the world to redeem my people. Behold, *I am Jesus Christ* . . . And never have I showed myself unto man whom I have created, for never has man believed in me as thou hast" (Ether 3:13-15). That is to say: "Never has there been such a complete and direct revelation of the nature and kind of being that I am."

While Mahonri beheld the spirit body of the Son of the Eternal Father, he was instructed: "Behold, this body which ye now behold, is the body of my spirit . . . and even as I appear unto thee to be in the spirit will I appear unto my people in the flesh" (Ether 3:16).

Moroni then adds these comments: "Jesus showed himself unto this man in the spirit, even after the manner and in the likeness of the same body even as he showed himself unto the Nephites. And he administered unto him even as he ministered unto the Nephites; and all this, that this man might know that he was God, because of the many great works which the Lord had showed unto him" (Ether 3:17-18).

Emer: "Omer began to be old; nevertheless, in his old age he begat Emer; and he anointed Emer to be king to reign in his stead" (Ether 9:14). "And Emer did execute judgment in righteousness all his days" (Ether 9:21). After anointing his son, Coriantum, to be king, Emer "lived four years, and he saw peace in the land; yea, and *he even saw the Son of Righteousness*, and did rejoice and glory in his day; and he died in peace" (Ether 9:22).

Lehi and his son, Nephi: In vision, both saw "the mother of the Son of God, after the manner of the flesh." After she had been carried away in the Spirit, she was "bearing a child in her arms. And the angel said unto [Nephi]: *Behold the Lamb of God, yea, even the Son of the Eternal Father!"* (1 Nephi 11:1-6, 18-21). In addition, they saw the baptism, ministry, and crucifixion of the Lamb of God (1 Nephi 11: 24-33). Though Lehi and Nephi saw the mortal Son of God, and aspects of his mortal ministry, Jesus Christ was not yet born in mortality when this vision was given. Therefore, it is placed in this chapter with those who saw the premortal Lord.

THE ETERNAL FATHER AND HIS SON

Nephi and his brother Jacob: "And now I, Nephi, write more of the words of Isaiah . . . for he verily saw my Redeemer, *even as I have seen him.* And my brother, *Jacob, also has seen him* . . ." (2 Ne.11: 2-3).

Lamoni: After hearing the words of Ammon, king Lamoni believed and fell to the ground as if he were dead. The next day, Lamoni arose and he "stretched forth his hand unto [his wife, the queen], and said: Blessed be the name of God, and blessed art thou. For as sure as thou livest, behold, *I have seen my Redeemer;* and he shall come forth, and be born of a woman, and he shall redeem all mankind who believe on his name" (Alma 19:6-13).

Alma: Alma, the son of Alma, said: "*Ye, methought I saw,* even as our father Lehi saw, *God sitting upon his throne*, surrounded with numberless concourses of angels, in the attitude of singing and praising their God . . ."(Alma 36:22).

MORONI

We conclude with a tender but powerful testimony of the last Nephite prophet. "And now I, Moroni, bid farewell unto the Gentiles, yea, and also unto my brethren whom I love, until we shall meet before the judgment-seat of Christ, where all men shall know that my garments are not spotted with your blood. *And then shall ye know that I have seen Jesus, and that he hath talked with me face to face*, and that he told me in plain humility, even as a man telleth another in mine own language, concerning these things; And only a few have I written, because of my weakness in writing. And now, I would commend you to seek this Jesus of whom the prophets and apostles have written, that the grace of God the Father, and also the Lord Jesus Christ, and the Holy Ghost, which beareth record of them, may be and abide in you forever. Amen" (Ether 12: 38-41).

To help explain how all of these righteous individuals saw the premortal Lord, we again rely upon the words of Moroni. "For it was by faith that Christ showed himself unto our fathers . . . and he showed not himself unto them until after they had faith in him; wherefore, it must needs be that some had faith in him, for he showed himself not unto the world . . .

"For if there be no faith among the children of men God can do no miracle before them; wherefore he showed not himself until after their faith" (Ether 12:7, 12).

It is important to emphasize that faith and righteousness go hand in hand. By righteous living, and exercising sufficient faith, men and women are able to see the Lord.

14

WHO HAS SEEN THE RESURRECTED LORD?—
MARY MAGDALENE AND MANY OTHERS

The first mortal to see the risen Lord was Mary Magdalene. According to the chronology we are using, it was Sunday, April 8, A.D. 33 when this glorious event transpired.[162] From John's record, we are informed that "early" in the morning, "when it was yet dark," Mary came to the tomb where Jesus was buried. Her mission was one of pure love and devotion. There at the tomb, she saw that the stone was "taken away from the sepulchre" (John 20:1). From the original writings of John, we are given further information. In addition to noticing that that the stone was taken away, she also saw "two angels sitting thereon" (JST John 20:1). Though we are not informed, we may suppose that she looked in and saw that the tomb was empty. With great concern, she ran first to Peter, then to John, and exclaimed, "They have taken away the Lord out of the sepulchre, and we know not where they have laid him" (John 20:2).

From the words spoken by Mary, Peter and John were fearful that someone had stolen the body of Jesus. Without hesitation, "they ran both together" to the tomb. John, who evidently was younger and swifter, "did outrun Peter, and came first to the sepulchre." He stooped down, "and looking in, saw the linen clothes lying" in the tomb; "yet went he not in" (John 20:3-5).

Without hesitation, Simon Peter—the dynamic man of action—rushed into the sepulchre. John then entered. Together they saw the grave clothes, and "the napkin, that was about [Jesus'] head, not lying with the linen clothes, but wrapped together in a place by itself." After seeing the burial clothes, John wrote that he "believed." Giving explanation about himself and his fellow apostles believing: "For as yet they knew not the scripture, that he must rise again from the dead." That is, they had not known before, but they now knew that Christ was risen from the dead. After seeing these things at the tomb, the two apostles went "unto their own homes" (John 20:6-10).

Because of her devotion, Mary Magdalene returned to the tomb. There, she "stood without at the sepulchre weeping." While this faithful woman still "wept, she stooped down, and looked in the sepulcher." We can imagine her surprise, for she saw "two angels in white" clothing, "sitting, the one at the head, and the other of the feet, where the body of Jesus had lain" (John 20:10-12). Presumably they were the same angels who Mary first saw sitting on the stone that had covered the entrance to the sepulcher.

Kindly, the angles asked, "Woman, why weepest thou?"

With concern in her voice, Mary answered, "Because they have taken away my Lord, and I know not where they have laid him" (John 20:13).

Evidently she sensed that someone was standing near her, for as the record says, "she turned herself back" from the entrance of the tomb, "and saw Jesus standing, and knew not that it was Jesus."

Jesus said to her, "Woman, why weepest thou? whom seekest thou?"

Supposing him to be the gardener, she emotionally replied, "Sir, if thou have borne him hence, tell me where thou hast laid him, and I will take him away" (John 20:14-15).

With the Twelve Apostles, and other devoted disciples, Mary had traveled on many missionary journeys with the Son of God. Therefore, this faithful woman knew what Jesus looked like, and was familiar with the sound of his voice.

At the tomb, emotionally distraught and with eyes full of tears, Mary did not recognize Jesus, either by his looks or by his voice. Once again, the resurrected Lord spoke her name, "Mary." This time, she instantly recognized that familiar voice—even the voice of her beloved Jesus.

"One word from His loving lips changed her agonizing grief into ecstatic joy . . .," says Elder James E. Talmage, "The voice, the tone, the tender accent she had heard and loved in the earlier days lifted her from the despairing depths into which she had sunk." [163]

With joyful exuberance, Mary said, "Rabboni; which is to say, Master" (John 20:16). By sight and sound, Mary knew that Christ had risen from the dead.

After this transpired, Mary went to the Apostles and told them what had happened. Then, this blessed woman bore her testimony that "she had seen the Lord" (John 20:18).

"For reasons of his own," says Elder McConkie, "the risen Lord singled out Mary Magdalene to be the first witness . . . of his resurrection. She was the first mortal of all mortals ever to see a resurrected person. [164]

OTHER WOMEN

In addition to *Mary Magdalene*, Jesus chose to appear to and be touched by a group of other favored women. This group consisted of the following individuals:

Mary: The mother of James and Joses (Mark 15:40; Matt. 27:56).

Joanna: Who is presumed to be the wife of Chuza, Herod's steward (Luke 8:3).

Solome: The sister of Jesus' mother, Mary,[165] and the mother of the apostles James and John (Matt. 27:56; Mark 15:40).

With these four, there were "other women" who had been with Jesus in Galilee (Luke 24:1, 10; Mark 15:40-41). In speaking of this group, Elder McConkie says: "Certainly the beloved sisters from Bethany [Mary and Martha] were there; and, in general, the group would have been made up of the same ones who had [gathered] in sorrow around the cross. Their total number may well have been in the dozens . . ." [166] Later in his writing, he writes: "Certainly among those faithful sisters there were some or all of the wives of the apostles; perhaps also there were sisters or even daughters." [167]

After seeing and hearing the two angels at the empty tomb, the women "departed quickly from the sepulchre with . . . great joy; and did run to bring his [Jesus'] disciples word" (Matt. 28:5-8; JST Matt. 28:4; JST Mark 16:3; JST Luke 24:2, 4).

"And as they went to tell his disciples, behold, Jesus met them, saying, *All hail*." These faithful women immediately recognized the Lord, and his familiar voice. In reverence, "they came and held him by the feet, and worshipped him" (Matt. 28:9).

PETER, THE CHIEF APOSTLE

At the tomb, the women were told by the angels: "Be not affrighted: Ye seek Jesus of Nazareth, which was crucified: he is risen; he is not here: behold the place where they laid him.

"But go your way, tell his disciples and *Peter* that he goeth before you into Galilee: there shall ye see him, as he said unto you." (Mark 16:6-7; JST Mark 16:4-5)

"This use of Peter's name," says Elder McConkie, "leaves an added witness that he was called to preside over the Twelve and the church and was expected to lead out in governing the affairs of the earthly kingdom . . . ."[168]

Though we do not know when or where, we know that our Lord appeared to the senior apostle.[169] From Luke, we find that when the "eleven" apostles were gathered together—including Peter—with other members in a Church meeting, testimony was borne that "The Lord is risen indeed, and hath *appeared to Simon*" (Luke 24:33-34).

Later, Paul writes: "That Christ died for our sins . . . And that he was buried, and that he rose again the third day according to the scriptures: And that he was seen of *Cephas*, then of the twelve" (1 Cor. 15:5, italics added). Regarding Paul using the name of "*Cephas*," we are informed that when Peter first met the Messiah, Jesus said: "Thou are Simon the son of Jona: thou shalt be called Cephas, which is by interpretation, a stone" (John 1:42).

We, therefore, have two New Testament testimonies recorded that Simon Peter, the Rock and the Seer, saw the resurrected Lord. Though we do not know what was spoken at these appearances, we may be assured that our resurrected Lord spoke words of comfort and counsel to his senior apostle.

CLEOPAS AND LUKE

Probably, it was the afternoon of the day of our Lord's resurrection when two disciples left Jerusalem and walked the road to Emmaus. The one is identified as Cleopas; the other is unnamed (Luke 24:18). Various scholars have concluded that the unnamed disciple is Luke, for he vividly records the personal details of the visit with the resurrected Christ.

As these two men walked, they spoke of the Lord, his death, and teachings concerning his resurrection. While these disciples were talking, "Jesus himself drew near, and went with them" (Luke 24:15). By laws not revealed, Jesus hid his identity. The record says: "But their eyes were holden that they should not know him" (Luke 24:16; See also Mark 16:12). The Joseph Smith Translation makes this significant addition: "But their eyes were holden, *or covered,* that they *could* not know him" (JST Luke 24:15).

After spending considerable time talking of events that had recently transpired, including the visit by the women to the sepulchre, Jesus "expounded unto them in all the scriptures the things concerning himself" (Luke 24:27).

As these three neared Emmaus, Jesus "made as though" he would travel on. Because they desired to speak further with this stranger, the two disciples said, "Abide with us: for it is toward evening, and the day is far spent." Jesus consented. As they sat, "he took bread, and blessed it, and brake, and gave to them" (Luke 24:28-30).

Finally, the disciples' "eyes were opened, and they knew him; and he vanished out of their sight" (Luke 24:31). The Joseph Smith Translation of Luke says: "And their eyes were opened, and they knew him; and he *was* taken up out of their sight" (JST Luke 24:15, 30).

These two disciples were blessed to see the resurrected Lord and converse with him for an extended time. They quickly returned to Jerusalem to tell others. "And they told what things *they saw and heard* in the way, and how he [the Lord] was known *to* them . . ." (JST Luke 24:34).

TEN APOSTLES AND OTHER DISCIPLES

After Cleopas and Luke had concluded telling the apostles and other disciples what they had seen and heard, "Jesus himself stood in the midst of them," and said, "Peace be unto you." The doors were shut because of their fear of the Jews (John 20:19).

Though Luke wrote that eleven apostles were present (Luke 24:33), we learn that only ten of the twelve were there. The reason only ten were present is as follows: Judas Iscariot had committed suicide (Matt. 27:3-5). For some unexplained reason, Thomas was not present (John 20:24).

Because Jesus suddenly appeared in the enclosed room, those in attendance "were terrified and affrighted, and supposed that they had seen a spirit."

Jesus spoke these assuring words: "Why are ye troubled? And why do thoughts arise in your hearts? Behold my hands and my feet, that it is I myself: handle me, and see; for a spirit hath not flesh and bones, as ye see me have (Luke 24:36-39). After this invitation, we may suppose that many came forward, if not all. Jesus then asked, "Have ye any meat?" (Luke 24:41).

Those present—both men and women, and probably some children—were eating an evening meal and, we may add, were holding a testimony meeting as they ate. Their meal included broiled fish and honeycomb. To demonstrate that he was capable of eating food as a resurrected being, Jesus "took it, and did eat before them" (Luke 24: 42-43).

How many individuals were in this meeting, we are not told. Truly this was a special occasion for those present to see the risen Lord, and to see and feel his resurrected body.

John provides this added information of what was said directly to the apostles: "Then said Jesus to them again, Peace be unto you: as my Father hath sent me, even so send I you" (John 20:21).

THOMAS AND HIS FELLOW APOSTLES

A week later, Thomas was present with the other apostles. Not accepting the words of his fellow servants that they had "seen the Lord," he said to them, "Except I shall see in his hands the print of the nails, and put my finger into the print of the nails, and thrust my hand into his side, I will not believe" (John 20:24-25).

Once again in the upper room, the doors were shut and probably guarded. As happened a week earlier, Jesus appeared "and stood in the midst, and said, Peace be unto you."

Looking at his doubting apostle, Jesus commanded: "Reach hither thy finger, and behold my hands; and reach hither thy hand, and thrust it into my side: and be not faithless, but believing" (John 20:26-27).

After obeying, Thomas no longer doubted that Jesus was resurrected and had a tangible body of flesh and bones. In reverent awe, he exclaimed: "My Lord and my God" (John 20:28).

Jesus replied: "Thomas, because thou hast seen me, thou hast believed: blessed are they that have not seen, and yet have believed" (John 20:29).

MORE THAN 500 BRETHREN

There was a commandment of the apostles to meet Jesus on a mountain in Galilee according to a previous appointment (Matt. 28:16). In addition to the eleven apostles, we are told that on this mountain, the resurrected Lord "was seen of above 500 brethren at once . . ." (1 Cor. 15:6). Here, Jesus reiterates gospel teachings, as well as sends his messengers forth to proclaim his gospel to "all nations" (Matt. 28:18-20; Mark 16:15-18).

JAMES, THE LORD'S BROTHER

Paul informs us that Jesus appeared to his own blood brother "James," who also became a member of the Twelve Apostles (1 Cor. 15:7; Gal. 1:19). Other than this statement, we have no written account of this appearance or what was said.

UNMENTIONED INDIVIDUALS

Elder McConkie has penned these persuasive words:

> We must not leave this part of our discussion without recording that, without question, there were many unmentioned appearances. We know He was with them, from time to time, for forty days; and it is unthinkable to assume that he did not appear to the Blessed Virgin [Mary] whose Son he was, to Lazarus whom he called forth from four days of death, to Mary and Martha whom he loved, and to hosts of others ... But it is not the time or the place that matters; rather, it is the reality of the appearances and the fact that it was clearly his purpose to manifest himself to all who prepared themselves to stand in the Divine Presence."[170]

STEPHEN, THE MARTYR

Among the "seven men of honest report" who were set apart under the hands of the apostles was Stephen (Acts 6: 2-5). Accused of "blasphemous words against Moses, and against God" (Acts 6:11), Stephen was brought before the supreme council of the Sanhedrin. After recounting the history of Israel and naming Moses as a prototype of Christ, the Sanhedrin were maddened at his comments. At this time, Stephen knew that they thirsted for his blood. He looked up and declared, "Behold I see the heavens opened, and the Son of man standing on the right hand of God" (Acts 7:56).

Elder Talmage states: "This is the first New Testament record of a manifestation of Christ to mortal eyes by vision ..." [171]

The Sanhedrin rushed upon Stephen and took him out of the city and stoned him to death (Acts 7:57-60). Accordingly, Stephen became the first martyr sharing his testimony of the risen Christ, after our Lord ascended to his Father.

SAUL, KNOWN AS PAUL

Concerning Saul, Elder Talmage has written of him: "Saul was a violent opponent of the apostles and the Church, and had made himself a party to the death of Stephen by openly consenting thereunto and by holding in personal custody the garments of the false witnesses while they stoned the martyr." (Acts 7:58; 8:1).[172]

After a miraculous conversion (Acts 9:3-29; 22:6-16; 26:12-18), he became a valiant defender of the gospel of Jesus Christ. "His Hebrew name, Saul, was in time substituted by the Latin Paulus, or as to us, Paul" (Acts 13:9).[173]

While in Jerusalem, Paul was blessed with a visual manifestation of the Lord, accompanied by receiving specific instructions. "And it came to pass, that, when I was come again to Jerusalem, even while I prayed in the temple, I was in a trance; and saw him [the Lord] saying unto me, Make haste, and get thee quickly out of Jerusalem: for they will not receive thy testimony concerning me" (Acts 22:17-18).

"Once again," says Elder Talmage, "as he lay a prisoner in the Roman castle, the Lord stood by him in the night, and said: 'Be of good cheer, Paul: for as thou hast testified of me in Jerusalem, so must thou bear witness also at Rome' (Acts 23:11).

"Paul's personal witness that he had seen the resurrected Christ is explicit and emphatic."[174] Lastly, in speaking of various appearances of the resurrected Lord, Paul wrote: "And last of all he was seen of me also . . . For I am the least of the apostles, that am not meet to be called an apostle, because I persecuted the church of God" (1 Cor. 15:8-9).

JOHN, THE REVELATOR

After he became a translated being,[175] John was eventually banished to the isle of Patmos (John 21:18-25; D&C 7:4-8;

Rev.1:9). Elder Talmage writes: "The apostle gives a vivid description of the glorified Christ as seen by him; and of the Lord's words . . ."[176] (Rev. 1:10-20).

NEPHITE MULTITUDE

As discussed in Chapter 10, the resurrected Lord appeared to the Nephite multitude. We know that he appeared twice to this blessed people, chose the Nephite Twelve, and because of their faith and desire, he allowed three of the Twelve to become translated beings (3 Nephi 11-29).[177]

We are not informed of how many people saw the Lord during this glorious time, but Elder McConkie has written these plausible words: "Thereafter came the Nephite ministry during which thousands upon thousands (we suppose tens and scores of thousands) heard his voice, felt the nail marks in his hands and feet, thrust their hands into his side, and (many of them) wet his feet with their tears."[178]

LOST TRIBES OF ISRAEL

While speaking to the Nephite multitude, Jesus said: "But now I go unto the Father, and also to show myself unto the lost tribes of Israel, for they are not lost unto the Father, for he knoweth whither he hath taken them" (3 Nephi 17:4). Again, we use the words of Elder McConkie: "He also visited the Lost Tribes of the house of Israel and did for them, as we suppose, what he had done for others."[179]

From these various accounts, we know that the resurrected Lord appeared to countless numbers of individuals. Truly, these manifestations prove that he rose from the dead; and like his Father, Jesus has a resurrected body of flesh and bones (D&C 130:22).

15

WHO HAS SEEN THE LORD IN OUR DAY?—
(JUNE 9, 1830 THROUGH SEPT. 2, 1898)

NEWEL KNIGHT

As discussed in Chapter 12, during the last week in May, 1830, Newel Knight came to Fayette, New York and was baptized by David Whitmer. On the ninth of June, 1830, the first Conference of the Church was held.[180] While at this Conference, Newel Knight saw heaven open and beheld *the Lord Jesus Christ*, seated on the right hand of the Father. Following this experience, Brother Knight rehearsed to the Prophet Joseph Smith the glorious things which he had seen and felt, while he was in the spirit.[181]

LYMAN WIGHT

At a Conference of the Church held June 3-6, 1831, the Spirit of the Lord came upon the Prophet Joseph Smith and he prophesied various things. Concluding his remarks, the Prophet laid his hands upon Lyman Wight and ordained him a High Priest. Following this ordination, the spirit of the Lord fell came upon Brother Wight and he prophesied concerning the coming of Christ. At the conclusion of his remarks, Lyman *saw the heavens opened and the Son of Man* sitting on the right hand of the Father, making intercession for his brethren, the Saints.[182]

JOSEPH SMITH, JR. AND MARTIN HARRIS

In the early summer of 1831, Mary Elizabeth Rollins, a twelve-year-old girl visited the Prophet Joseph Smith's home in Kirtland, Ohio with her mother. Mary wanted to learn more about the Book of Mormon. Other unmentioned friends and relatives were there as well. When the Prophet entered the room, he suggested a meeting be held. Miss Rollins recalls:

> After praying and singing, Joseph began talking. He began very solemnly and earnestly. Suddenly he stopped and seemed almost transfixed, he was looking ahead and his face outshone the candle which was on the shelf just behind him. I thought I could almost see his cheekbones. He looked as though a searchlight was inside his face and shining through every pore. I could not take my eyes from his face . . . After a short time he looked at us very solemnly, and said, *'Brothers and Sisters, do you know who has been in your midst this night?'* One of the Smith family said: 'An angel of the Lord.' Joseph did not answer. Martin Harris was sitting at the Prophet's feet on a box, he slid to his knees, clasped his arms around the Prophet's knees and said, "I know, it was our Lord and Saviour Jesus Christ." Joseph put his hand on Martin's head and answered, "Martin, God revealed that to you. Brothers and Sisters, *the Saviour has been in your midst,* I want you

to remember it. He cast a veil over your eyes for you could not endure to look upon Him. You must fed with milk and not meat. I want you to remember this as if it were the last thing that escapes my lips." [183]

JOHN MURDOCK

"During the winter of 1832-33," John Murdock, "boarded with the Prophet [Joseph Smith] in Kirtland. A number of prayer meetings were held in which they obtained great blessings. John Murdock records in his Journal:

"'In one of those meetings *the Prophet told us if we would humble ourselves before God, and exercise strong faith, we should see the face of the Lord.* And about midday the visions of my mind were opened, and the eyes of my understanding were enlightened, and *I saw the form of a man,* most lovely; the visage of His face was round and fair as the sun; His hair a bright silver grey, curled in most majestic form; His eyes a keen penetrating blue; and the skin of His neck a most beautiful white. He was covered from the neck to the feet with a loose garment of pure white—whiter than any garment I had ever before seen. His countenance was most penetrating, and yet most lovely. And while I was endeavoring to comprehend the whole personage from head to feet it slipped from me, and the vision was closed. But it left on my mind the impression of love, for months, that I never before felt to that degree."[184]

JOSEPH SMITH JR., AND SIDNEY RIGDON

As discussed in Chapter 12, Joseph Smith, Jr. alone saw both the Father and the Son in the year 1820. Following the organization of the Church, on April 6, 1830, the Prophet Joseph Smith received various revelations from the Lord.

THE ETERNAL FATHER AND HIS SON

In one of the most remarkable visions given in mortality, the Prophet Joseph Smith and Sidney Rigdon saw and conversed with Jesus Christ, the Son of the Eternal Father, on February 16, 1832. This revelation was received shortly after the Prophet returned to Hiram, Ohio, from the Amherst, Conference, where he had been sustained as President of the High Priesthood.[185]

Included in this revelation are these words: "We, Joseph Smith, Jun., and Sidney Rigdon, being in the Spirit on the sixteenth day of February, in the year of our Lord one thousand eight hundred and thirty-two—By the power of the Spirit our eyes were opened and our understandings were enlightened, so as to see and understand the things of God—Even those things which were from the beginning before the world was, which were ordained of the Father, through his Only Begotten Son, who was in the bosom of the Father, even from the beginning; Of whom we bear record; and the record which we bear is the fulness of the gospel of *Jesus Christ, who is the Son, whom we saw and with whom we conversed in the heavenly vision*" (D&C 76:11-14, italics added).

Both Joseph and Sidney are humbly declaring that they saw and spoke with Jesus Christ. They further state in this vision: "And *we beheld the glory of the Son, on the right hand of the Father* . . ." (D&C 76:20).

Further: "And now, after the many testimonies which have been given of him, this is the testimony, last of all, which we give of him: That he lives!

"*For we saw him, even on the right hand of God;* and we heard the voice bearing record that he is the Only Begotten of the Father . . ." (D&C 76:22-23).

AT THE NEWLY COMPLETED KIRTLAND TEMPLE

Also discussed in Chapter 12, on January 21, 1836, the first meeting was held in the newly completed Kirtland Temple.[186] In attendance were the Presidency of the Church and Joseph Smith, Sr., the Patriarch of the Church. At this first meeting, the Presidency gave the Patriarch a blessing; then the Patriarch gave the members of the Presidency a blessing.[187] Following these blessings, the Prophet Joseph Smith received the following vision:

"The heavens were opened upon us, and I beheld the celestial kingdom of God, and the glory thereof . . Also the blazing throne of God, *whereon was seated the Father and the Son . . .*[188] (D&C 137: 1-3).

AT THE SAME MEETING

At this same meeting, Thursday, January 21, 1836, various councils and presiding officers in the several quorums, each in turn, received blessings by the anointing of oil and laying on of hands. The visions of heaven were opened to their view. *Some of them saw the face of the Savior*, and others were ministered unto by holy angels . . .[189]

JOSEPH SMITH, JR. AND ZEBEDEE COLTRIN— 1833

As noted previously, Brother Zebedee Coltrin is quoted as saying: "I believe I am the only living man now in the Church who was connected with the School of the Prophets when it was organized in 1833.[190] (See D&C 88:127; 90:7, 13).

"Every time we were called together to attend to any business, we came together in the morning about sunrise, fasting, and partook of the Sacrament each time; and before going to school we washed ourselves and put on clean linen. At one of those meetings after the organization of the school . . . on the 23 of January, 1833, when we were all together, [the Prophet] Joseph having given instructions, and while engaged in silent prayer, kneeling, with our hands uplifted, each one praying in silence, no one whispered above his breath, *a personage walked through the room from East to West, and Joseph asked if we saw him.* I [Zebedee] saw him and suppose the others did, and Joseph answered that is *Jesus, the Son of God, our elder brother . . ."*[191]

ZEBEDEE COLTRIN—1836

On Thursday, January 28, 1836, at a meeting in the Kirtland Temple, with the Prophet Joseph Smith present, *President Zebedee Coltrin, one of the seven presidents of the Seventy, saw the Savior* . . .[192]

PRESIDENT FREDERICK G. WILLIAMS

Frederick G. Williams was called by revelation, March, 1832, to be a "high priest" in the Church, "and a counselor" to the Prophet Joseph Smith (D&C 81:1). The following was not recorded by the Prophet in his History, but was related by Elder George A. Smith in 1864: "On the first day of the dedication" [of the Kirtland Temple], President Frederick G. Williams, one of the Council of the Prophet, and who occupied the upper pulpit, *bore testimony that the Savior,* dressed in his vesture without seam, came into the stand and accepted of the dedication of the house, *that he saw him,* and gave a description of his clothing and all things pertaining to it."[193]

BRUCE E. DANA

JOSEPH SMITH JR., AND OLIVER COWDREY

The Kirtland Temple was dedicated by President Joseph Smith on Sunday, March 27, 1836 (D&C 109).[194] A week later, Sunday, April 3, 1836, in the Kirtland Temple, Presidents Joseph Smith and Oliver Cowdery went to the west pulpit to engage in silent prayer.[195] In the Kirtland Temple there were two seating stands. The west end was reserved for the presiding officers of the Melchizedek Priesthood; the east end was for the Aaronic Priesthood. Each stand had two pulpits, rising above the other. Each of these pulpits could be separated from the others by veils of painted canvas, which could be let down or rolled up as desired.[196]

In the afternoon, the Prophet says that he assisted in seating the congregation, which consisted of "about one thousand persons." After the sacrament was administered, Joseph Smith and Oliver Cowdery went "to the pulpit," at the west end of the temple. After "the veils" were lowered, both offered a "solemn and silent prayer." After rising from prayer, the following vision was given to them:[197]

> The veil was taken from our minds, and the eyes of our understanding were opened. *We saw the Lord standing upon the breastwork of the pulpit, before us;* and under his feet was a paved work of pure gold, in color like amber. His eyes were as a flame of fire; the hair of his head was white like the pure snow; his countenance shone above the brightness of the sun; and his voice was as the sound of the rushing of great waters, even the voice of Jehovah, saying: I am the first and the last; I am he who liveth, I am he who was slain; I am your advocate with the Father . . .[198] (D&C 110:1-4).

Thus, Joseph and Oliver were blessed to see the Savior together. We are most grateful that their testimonies have been preserved as revelations, declaring to the world that they saw and conversed with God's Son in these the latter-days.

UNNAMED BRETHREN SAW THE SAVIOR

On Wednesday, April 30, 1836, at eight o'clock that evening, the Presidency of the Church, the Twelve Apostles, the Seventies, the High Council, the Bishops and their entire quorums, the Elders, and all of the official members in the stake in Kirtland, Ohio met in the Kirtland Temple to attend to the ordinance of washing of feet. This congregation amounted to about three hundred men.

Addressing these brethren, the Prophet said that they probably should not leave this place until morning. In addition, he told those present that he had completed the organization of the Church, and that they had passed through all the necessary ceremonies, and had received from him all the instructions they needed, and that after obtaining their licenses, they were at liberty to go and build up the Kingdom of God.

He further said that because the Presidency had spent the previous night in the temple waiting upon the Lord, that they would leave, but those in attendance were to tarry all night and worship before the Lord. The Prophet left the meeting in charge of the Twelve Apostles, and he retired around nine o'clock that evening.

The brethren in attendance continued exhorting, prophesying, and speaking in tongues until five o'clock in the morning. Then, *the Savior made His appearance to some*, while angels ministered to others . . .[199]

Someday, perhaps, we hope to learn who the Savior appeared to, and whether any counsel or instruction was spoken. This truly was a "day of Pentecost," for those brethren in the Kirtland Temple.

ALFRED DOUGLAS YOUNG

As stated earlier, Alfred Douglas Young was an early convert of the Church. While conversing with his brother on the morning of September 17, 1841, concerning the principles of the gospel, he was prompted by the Spirit to go to some secret place. He went to the woods near his brother's home, and an angel beckoned him in vision by saying, "Follow thou me."

Concerning this angelic personage, Brother Young says: "He ascended upward in the direction from whence he came and I followed him. *He took me* into the presence of God the Father *and his Son Jesus Christ.* There was a rail between us; but I saw them seated on a throne."

Later, he wrote: "While I prayed the rail was removed and I stood upon my feet. *Jesus arose* and stepped from the side of his Father and came near where I stood. *I was in their presence and I gazed upon their glory. . .*"[200]

ALEXANDER NEIBAUR

Alexander Neibaur, a Jewish convert from England and a dental surgeon by profession, was asked by his son shortly before his death: "'Father you have been telling us of your long and hard experience, and we have listened with intense affection and interest. But let me ask you, is it worth it all? Is the gospel worth all this sacrifice?'

"The flow of testimony and of truth lighted the torches in the dimming eyes of the ancient Hebrew prophet and poet (Brother Neibaur) and he lifted his voice in firm and lofty assurance as he said:

> Yes! Yes! And more! *I have seen my Savior.* I have seen the prints in his hands! I know that Jesus is the Son of God, and I know that this work is true and that Joseph

Smith was a prophet of God. I would suffer it all and more, far more than I have ever suffered for that knowledge even to the laying down of my body on the plains for the wolves to devour."[201]

PRESIDENT GEORGE Q. CANNON

George Q. Cannon was ordained an apostle on August 26, 1860, age 33, by President Brigham Young. President Cannon was sustained as First Counselor to President Wilford Woodruff on April 7, 1889.

Under a heading of April 20, 1893, it is written: "President George Q. Cannon said, '*I have seen the Saviour, Jesus Christ, and conversed with Him face to face and He has talked with me.*'"[202]

In another publication, the following is written: "In a discourse of George Q. Cannon given in the Celestial Room of the newly dedicated Salt Lake Temple, he bore his testimony that God and his Son Jesus do live, *that he has seen and conversed with Jesus as one man with another.*"[203]

Lastly, we read the words of President Cannon: "I know that this is the work of God. *I know that God lives. I know that Jesus lives; for I have seen Him*. I know that this is the Church of God, and that it is founded on Jesus Christ, our Redeemer. I testify to you of these things *as one that knows*—as one of the Apostles of the Lord Jesus Christ that can bear witness to you today in the presence of the Lord *that he lives* and that He will live, and will come to reign on the earth, to sway an undisputed scepter."[204]

PRESIDENT WILFORD WOODRUFF

"President W. Woodruff told some of the Saints that *our Saviour had appeared unto him in the East Room in the Holy of Holies*, and told him that he had accepted of the Temple and of the dedication services, and that the Lord forgave us his Saints who had assisted in any manner towards the erection [of the Temple] were forgiven us by the Lord Jesus Christ. He [God's Son] said . . . seek for the Spirit of God and we shall triumph, that if the Saints would be faithful their sins should be blotted out." [205] (Italics added).

PRESIDENT LORENZO SNOW

President Lorenzo Snow, who then was President of the Quorum of Twelve Apostles, saw the resurrected Lord. The following account was written by LeRoi C. Snow, a son of President Snow:

> My father went to his room in the Salt Lake Temple, dressed in his robes of the Priesthood, knelt at the sacred alter in the Holy of Holies in the House of the Lord [Salt Lake Temple] and there plead to the Lord to spare President [Wilford] Woodruff's life, that President Woodruff might outlive him and that the great responsibility of Church leadership would not fall upon his shoulders. Yet he promised the Lord that he would devotedly perform any duty required at his hand. At this time he was in his eighty-sixth year. Soon after this President Woodruff was taken to [San Francisco,] California where he died Friday morning at 6:40 o'clock September 2, 1898. [President Woodruff was 91.] President Snow put on his holy temple robes, repaired again to the same sacred alter [in the Salt Lake Temple] . . . and poured out his heart to the Lord.

Then, this revealing information is written:

THE ETERNAL FATHER AND HIS SON

After finishing his prayer he expected a reply, some special manifestation from the Lord. So he waited,—and waited—and waited. There was no reply, no voice, no visitation, no manifestation. He left the altar and the room in great disappointment.

This next comment demonstrates that prayers—even with the senior Apostle on earth—are answered when and where the Lord wants them answered:

Passing through the Celestial room and out into the large corridor *a glorious manifestation was given President Snow* which I relate in the words of his granddaughter, Allie Young Pond . . .

One evening while I was visiting grandpa Snow in his room in the Salt Lake Temple, I remained until the door keepers had gone and the night-watchmen had not yet come in, so grandpa said he would take me to the main front entrance and let me out that way. He got his bunch of keys from his dresser. After we left his room and while we were still in the large corridor leading into the celestial room, I was walking several steps ahead of grandpa when he stopped me and said: "Wait a moment, Allie, I want to tell you something. *It was right here that the Lord Jesus Christ appeared to me at the time of the death of President Woodruff.* He [the Lord] instructed me to go right ahead and reorganize the First Presidency of the Church at once and not wait as had been done after the death of the previous presidents, and that I was to succeed President Woodruff . . . Then Grandpa came a step nearer and held out his left hand and said: '*He stood right here, about three feet above the floor.* It looked as though He stood on a plate of solid gold . . . Grandpa told me what a *glorious personage the Savior is* and described His hands, feet, countenance and beautiful white robes, all of which were of such a *glory of whiteness and brightness* that he could hardly gaze upon Him . . . Then he [President

Snow] came another step nearer and put his right hand on my head and said: "Now, grand-daughter, I want you to remember that this is the testimony of your grand-father, that he told you with his own lips *that he actually saw the Savior, here in the Temple, and talked with him face to face.*" [206]

16

WHO HAS SEEN THE LORD IN OUR DAY?—
(OCTOBER 3, 1918 THROUGH OCTOBER 1, 1989)

PRESIDENT JOSEPH F. SMITH

Concerning his glorious vision of the redemption of the dead, President Joseph F. Smith says: "On the third of October, in the year nineteen hundred and eighteen, I sat in my room pondering over the scriptures; And reflecting upon the great atoning sacrifice that was made by the Son of God, for the redemption of the world; And the great and wonderful love made manifest by the Father and the Son in the coming of the Redeemer of the world; That through his atonement, and by obedience to the principles of the gospel, mankind might be saved" (D&C 138:1-4).

President Smith goes on to say that his "mind reverted to the writings of the apostle Peter . . . I opened the Bible and read the third and fourth chapters of the first epistle of Peter . . ." (D&C 138:5-6).

"As I pondered over these things which are written, the eyes of my understanding were opened, and the Spirit of the Lord rested upon me, and I saw the hosts of the dead, both small and great. And there were gathered together in one place an innumerable company of the spirits of the just, who had been faithful in the testimony of Jesus while they lived in mortality . . . I beheld that they were filled with joy and gladness, and were rejoicing together because the day of their deliverance was at hand. They were assembled awaiting the advent of the Son God into the spirit world, to declare their redemption from the bands of death . . . (D&C 138:11-12, 15-16).

"While this vast multitude waited and conversed, rejoicing in the hour of their deliverance from the chains of death, *the Son of God appeared*, declaring liberty to the captives who had been faithful;

"And there he preached to them the everlasting gospel [the same gospel that Jesus also preached in mortality], the doctrine of the resurrection and the redemption of mankind from the fall, and from individual sins on conditions of repentance" (D&C 138:18-19, italics added).

Thus, President Smith saw in vision *the Son of God*, and his ministry among the righteous dead. This glorious vision of the redemption of the dead was witnessed 47 days prior to his death, November 19, 1918, at age 80.

ELDER MELVIN J. BALLARD

Elder Melvin J. Ballard was ordained an apostle on January 7, 1919, at age 45, by President Heber J. Grant. He died on July 30, 1939, at age 66, at Salt Lake City, Utah. The following experience is not dated:

> Away on the Fort Peck Reservation where I was doing missionary work . . . among the Indians . . . I found myself one evening in the dreams of the night, in that sacred building, the [Salt Lake] Temple. After a season of prayer and rejoicing, I was informed that I should have the privilege of entering into one of those rooms, *to meet a glorious Personage*, and as I entered the door, *I saw*, seated on a raised platform *the most glorious*

THE ETERNAL FATHER AND HIS SON

Being my eyes ever have beheld, or that I ever conceived existed in all the eternal worlds. As I approached to be introduced, *he arose and stepped towards me with extended arms, and he smiled as he softly spoke my name.* If I shall live to be a million years old, I shall never forget that smile. He took me into his arms and kissed me, pressed me to His bosom, and blessed me, until the marrow of my bones seemed to melt! When he had finished, I fell at his feet, and as I bathed them with my tears and kisses, I saw the prints of the nails in the feet of the Redeemer of the World. The feeling that I had in the presence of Him who hath all things in his hands, to have His love, His affection, and His blessings was such that if I ever can receive that of which I had but a foretaste, I would give all that I am, all that I ever hope to be, to feel what I then felt![207]

In the April General Conference of 1920, Elder Ballard bore this testimony: "I know, as well as I know that I live and look into your faces, that Jesus Christ lives, and he is the Redeemer of the world, that he arose from the dead with a tangible body . . . For in the visions of the Lord to my soul, I have seen Christ's face. I have heard his voice. I know that he lives, that he is the Redeemer of the world . . ." [208]

ELDER RULON S. WELLS

Rulon S. Wells was set apart as one of the First Seven Presidents of Seventy on April 5, 1893, at age 38, by President George Q. Cannon. In the April General Conference of the Church in 1940, he said: "When I went upon my first mission I was blessed by President Brigham Young. He laid his hands upon my head on the twenty-second day of October, 1875, and blessed me and ordained me a Seventy and set me apart for my first mission, which was in Switzerland and German."

Later he said: "While on my way to my mission field, crossing the ocean on the Steamship Dakota, I went down into the salon of the ship one day, and lay upon one of the cushioned benches surrounding the eating tables, where I fell asleep. While asleep *the Lord appeared to me in a dream and I saw Him standing before me*; and by His side was William W. Taylor, one of the other missionaries, a son of President John Taylor, a boy like myself going upon his first mission. He [William] stood by the side of the Savior, and the *Savior extended his hand to me and grasping my hand, holding it tight, looked at me in the face and said: 'Will you ever doubt again?'* Brother Taylor, who stood beside Him said: 'I believe that is enough for him.' *With that, the Lord let go of my hand and I awoke.*"

"That is only another instance of how the Lord has been training and preparing me for my life's ministry, and I know that this is His work." [209]

ELDER GEORGE F. RICHARDS

George F. Richards was ordained an Apostle on April 9, 1906, at age 45, by President Joseph F. Smith. In an October General Conference of the Church of 1946, he said: "More than forty years ago *I had a dream*, which I am sure was from the Lord. In this dream *I was in the presence of my Savior as he stood in mid-air*. He spoke no word to me, but my love for him was such that I have not words to explain. I know that no mortal man can love the Lord as I experienced that love for the Savior unless God reveals it unto him. *I would have remained in his presence*, but there was a power drawing me away from him, and as a result of that dream I had this feeling, that no matter what might be required at my hands, what the gospel might entail unto me, I would do what I should be asked to do, even to the laying down of my life.'" [210]

Elder LeGrand Richards was ordained an Apostle on April 10, 1952, at age 66, by President David O. McKay. The following was related by him:

THE ETERNAL FATHER AND HIS SON

In a letter to LeGrand Richards, his son, Elder George F. Richards wrote: "*My son, I had a wonderful dream last night. I dreamed that the Savior visited me. He took me in his arms and embraced me. The joy that filled my soul cannot be compared with the joy and the feeling that a man has toward a woman. I feel the meaning of the words of the song, 'I Need Thee Every Hour.'*" [211]

ELDER ORSON F. WHITNEY

Orson F. Whitney was ordained an Apostle on April 9, 1906, at age 50, by President Joseph F. Smith. The following was related by him:

"I dreamed that I was in the garden of Gethsemane. I saw the Savior and the three Apostles [Peter, James, and John] enter a little gate at the right into the garden, and I stood, as it were, in the background, or the foreground, of the picture, *which I beheld as plainly as I now see the faces of those before me.* They did not see me, but I saw them . . . He [Jesus] knelt there praying to God to give Him strength to perform His mission, to pass through the ordeal which was before Him, to drink of 'the bitter cup' prepared by His Father. As he called upon God in the agony of His soul and asked him if it were possible to let the cup pass from Him, the tears streamed down His cheeks, and gazing upon His mental agony, I was constrained to weep in unison with Him . . . Presently He arose and beckoned His Apostles to Him. Then the circumstances seemed to change. The scene remained as it was; but instead of being in time before the crucifixion, it now appeared to be after that event. I thought He was leaving the earth and taking these Apostles with Him. My heart was so drawn out to Him with love and sympathy for His great suffering that *I ran out from behind the tree where I had stood gazing upon the picture, and fell down at His feet, clasped His knees, and asked Him to take me with Him* . . . I shall never forget the look of indescribable tenderness, affection, and compassion with which He gazed down upon me as I knelt before Him. *He lifted me up and embraced me.* I could feel the very warmth of His bosom, against which I rested; and as He took me in His arms with all the tenderness of a father or and elder brother, He shook His head and said: 'No my son, your work is not finished; you must remain and perform your mission. These (pointing to His apostles) have finished their work and they can go with Me; but you must remain' . . . I was so anxious, I felt such a love for Him and a desire to be with Him, that I clung to Him and pleaded with Him to let me go. But He continued to shake His head. I then said: 'Promise me that when I have finished my life I will come to You at last' . . . Again he gazed with tenderness and compassion, and uttered these words in tones which pierced my very soul, *'That, my son, will depend entirely upon yourself.'* I awoke and it was morning, *but I knew that I had been gazing upon a vision, that God had indeed spoken to me*, and that He had told me the truth in plainness and simplicity. I saw that I, too, must awake, that I must not sleep upon my post, I must not consider any of the things of this world as of paramount importance to the mission which I was sent to perform as a servant of the Lord Jesus Christ. I have often reflected upon the wisdom of the answer which He gave me when He told me that it *would depend entirely upon myself.*"[212]

ELDER MARK E. PETERSEN

Mark E. Petersen was ordained an Apostles on April 20, 1944, at age 43, by President Heber J. Grant. The following is about him: "Not long ago, L. Harold Wright, former Arizona Temple president, recalled escorting Mark E. Peterson (then an apostle, now deceased) to the Arizona Temple during off-hours, at his request. Leaving the apostle alone, President Wright returned after the appointed half-hour. Elder Petersen, indicating the landing at the top of the stairs outside the celestial room, *said he had seen the Savior there just ten minutes before.*"[213]

PRESIDENT DAVID O. MCKAY

Apia, Samoa. May 10, 1921. "I . . . fell asleep, and beheld in vision something infinitely sublime. In the distance I beheld a beautiful white city. Though far away, yet I seemed to realize that trees with luscious fruit, shrubbery with gorgeously-tinted leaves, and flowers in perfect bloom abounded everywhere. The clear sky above seemed to reflect these beautiful shades of color. I then saw a great concourse of people approaching the city. Each one wore a white flowing robe, and white headdress. Instantly my attention seemed centered upon their Leader, and though I could see only the profile of his features and body, I recognized him at once as my Savior! The tint and radiance of his countenance were glorious to behold! There was a peace about him which seemed sublime— it was divine! The city, I understood, was his. It was the City Eternal; and the people following him were to abide there in peace and eternal happiness. But who are they? As if the Savior read my thoughts, he answered by pointing to a semicircle that then appeared above them, and on which are written in gold the words: 'These Are They Who Have Overcome The World—Who Have Truly Been Born Again!' When I awoke, it was breaking day over Apia harbor."[214]

In addition to this dream-vision, President David O. McKay, Second Counselor to President George Albert Smith, said in an April General Conference of the Church of 1949: "Brethren, I know as I know I am looking into your faces that the Gospel of Jesus Christ is true, and *that He is my Saviour,* as real as He was when Thomas said, with bowed head, 'My Lord and my God!'" [215] (See John 20:24-28, italics added).

Paraphrasing the words spoken by President McKay, W. Cleon Skousen wrote:

> "President David O. McKay cloaked his own marvelous manifestation by simply *saying that he had received the same testimony of the reality of Jesus Christ as Thomas, the doubting apostle.*" [216]

COMMENTS BY BOYD K. PACKER

In one of his published works, under a sub-title, *Too Sacred to Discuss,* Elder Boyd K. Packer wrote these revealing words:

"All teachers are, of course, themselves students. While as teachers there are some difficult questions that we can hardly attempt to answer, likewise as students there are some questions that we could not in propriety ask.

"One question of this type I am asked occasionally, usually by someone who is curious, is, *'Have you seen Him?'* That is a question that *I have never asked of another. I have not asked that question of my Brethren in the Council of the Twelve,* thinking that it would be so sacred and so personal that one would have to have some special inspiration—indeed, some authorization—even to ask it.

"Though I have not asked that question of others, *I have heard them answer it*—but not when they were asked. I have heard one of my Brethren declare, *'I know, from experiences too sacred to relate, that Jesus is the Christ.'* I have heard another testify, 'I know that God lives, I know that the Lord lives, and *more than that, I know the Lord.'* I repeat: they have answered this question not when they were asked, but under the promptings of the Spirit, on sacred occasions, when 'the Spirit beareth record'" (D&C 1:39). [217]

17

GOD IS OMNIPOTENT—
ATTRIBUTE OF POWER

In the Book of Mosiah, King Benjamin informs us that "an angel from heaven" spoke with him and said: "For behold, the time cometh, and is not far distant, that with *power*, the *Lord Omnipotent* who reigneth, who was, and is from all eternity to all eternity, shall come down from heaven among the children of men, and shall dwell in a tabernacle of clay [meaning: having a physical body] . . .

"And he shall be called Jesus Christ, the Son of God . . . the Creator of all things from the beginning; and his mother shall be called Mary . . ." (Mosiah 3:2, 5, 8).

In addition, John the Revelator said: "And I heard as it were the voice of a great multitude . . . saying, Allelulia: for the *Lord God omnipotent reigneth*" (Rev. 19:6).

Referencing these scriptures, Elder McConkie says "Christ is the Lord Omnipotent, *meaning that as Lord of all he has all power*." [218] He further writes that *"Omnipotence consists in having unlimited power, and God has all power, and there is no power which he does not have."* [219]

With another understanding, we turn to the expressions of

Elder B. H. Roberts: "By 'Omnipotence' is mall-powerfulness. This attribute is essential to all rational thinking upon God. We may not think upon God and then think upon him as being overruled by a higher power, and still have him remain to our thought as God. The scriptures in their whole spirit present this view of the Omnipotence of Deity . . ."

Later, he writes these persuasive and logical words: "The attribute 'Omnipotence' must needs be thought upon . . . *as somewhat limited.* Even God, notwithstanding the ascription to him of all-powerfulness in such scripture phrases as 'With God all things are possible' (See Matt. 19:26), 'Nothing shall be impossible with God' (See Luke 1:37)—notwithstanding all this, I say, not even God may have two mountain ranges without a valley between. Not even God may place himself beyond the boundary of space: nor on the outside of duration. Nor is it conceivable to human thought that he can create space, or annihilate matter. These are things that limit even God's omnipotence."[220]

From this explanation, we are made aware that God—even the Lord God Omnipotent—is limited in power by eternal existences and laws. All things are governed by law (D&C 88:42). Both the Father and Son govern by law; and we add, are governed by law (D&C 88:13). It is revealed: "Unto every kingdom is given a law; *and unto every law there are certain bounds also and conditions . . .*" (D&C 88:38).

With this understanding, we read the words of Elder Orson Pratt: "Every one knows that it is absurd to believe in a personage being present in two places at once. 'But,' says one, 'nothing is impossible with God.' But I beg to differ with such persons, and inform them, that if the Scripture be true, *there are things which are impossible with God . . .*"[221]

Both the Father and Son work by laws that have certain bounds and conditions. Though the Father and Son have great power, they are bound by law!

Elder Orson F. Whitney has said: "There is nothing possible

THE ETERNAL FATHER AND HIS SON

of achievement that God cannot do, *but there may be things that he has not time to do, and which may be done for him.* There are some things, however, that even God cannot do. I speak it with all reverence. For instance, He cannot make something out of nothing, though many pious Christians ascribe to Him that power—if such it can be called. There is another thing that God cannot do—he cannot be present in all places at the same time, in His own proper person. This is God's work, and it can only be done by the power of God; but we cannot expect Him to be everywhere present, nor in two places at the same time, except by His authority, His Spirit and His influence." [222]

By his delegation of authority, the Father uses the Son and the Holy Ghost to do many things for him. The Father and Son delegate authority Prophet, Seers, and Revelators to perform things on earth. Therefore, by the laws and ordinances of the gospel of Jesus Christ, mankind can be saved.

We conclude this section on God's omnipotence, by using the words of Elder James E. Talmage: "The thoughtless man says, 'God, being omnipotent, can do anything.' *I don't believe it.* There are many things that God can't do. And having thus far committed myself to what some may consider a heresy, I will go a step farther. There are many things that God can't do that you can do, and I can do. *He can't lie.* [See Heb. 6:18] Can you? He can't be unjust. Can we? Let the oppression of man by his brother, in the world today, answer! *God's omnipotence means that he can do anything that he wills to do, but he wills to do only that which is righteous, just, [and] holy!"* [223] And, we add, only that which is in accordance with eternal law!

OMNIPRESENCE—LIGHT OF CHRIST FILLS ALL SPACE

Concerning Jesus Christ, it is written: "He is above all things, and in all things, and is through all things, and is round about all things; and all things are by him, and of him, even God, forever and ever" (D&C 88:41).

"It is by reference to this true doctrine of *omnipresence*," says Elder McConkie, "that the sectarian world attempts to justify its false creeds which describe Deity as a vague, ethereal, immaterial essence which fills the immensity of space and is everywhere and nowhere in particular present." [224]

We know that the Father and Son are separate, resurrected Beings, with bodies of flesh and bones as tangible as man's (D&C 130:22). In harmony with this doctrine, we repeat what was previously written by Elder Whitney—"[God] cannot be present in all places at the same time, in His own proper person." [225]

The Light of Christ proceeds from the presence of God and fills the immensity of space, "The light which is in all things, which giveth life to all things, which is the law by which all things are governed, even the power of God who sitteth upon his throne, who is in the bosom of eternity, who is in the midst of all things" (D&C 88:12-13).

Concerning this scripture, Elder B. H. Roberts has expressed these words:

> I myself gather comfort from this one great thought— this immanent spirit, this ever-present God, in whom we live and move and have our being is called 'the light of Christ.' Why not the light of the Father? Because that Spirit proceeds forth from the presence of the Father as well as from the presence of the Son. Why not call it the light of the Father? Because, as I quoted to you near the beginning of this discourse, God was manifest in the flesh through Jesus Christ . . . [226]

To distinguish between Christ and the Light of Christ, Elder McConkie has further written: "The spirit which proceeds from his person to govern and control all that he has created is everywhere present and does fill the immensity of space. But this is

THE ETERNAL FATHER AND HIS SON

not God; it is the agency through which he works, the power that he has in all things!" [227]

In harmony with these teachings, we again use the words of Elder B. H. Roberts: "It is not then a personality in itself, that is in the sense of being of individual form, but proceeds forth from a personality; it is a presence rather than a person; an influence, a spiritual atmosphere, a power proceeding from another [who is Christ] . . ."

Later, he gives this explanation: "'The Light of Christ' will be the same or identical with the Light of the Father; and the light of all Intelligence who have participated in the divine nature and become one with the Father and the Son. *So that it might be properly held that the God Immanent is as much the 'Light of the Father' as 'The Light of Christ'; and since that light would be identical with the light of all perfected and holy beings, participating in the Divine nature, it could receive a name that would generate it—the 'Divine Spirit, Immanent in the Universe'* . . . any of these characterizations would doubtless be admissible; but since it is through the Christ that the Divine nature and spirit is manifested in our world, it is proper that this Divine Light which lighteth every man into the world . . . should bear the name of Christ—and henceforth we shall recognize it as our modern revelations do, primarily, as 'The Light of Christ.'" [228]

We further learn from Elder Joseph Fielding Smith that every person receives the Light of Christ. He says, "The Lord has not left men (when they are born into this world) helpless, groping to find the light and truth, but every man that is born into the world is born with the right to receive the guidance, the instruction, the counsel of the Spirit of Christ, or Light of Truth, sometimes called the Spirit of the Lord in our writings." [229]

In other words, the Light of Christ acts as our conscience so that every person knows, more or less, right from wrong. Elder Smith further explains that the "Light of Christ is not a personage.

It has no body." And, that it gives light to the sun and life to vegetation. (See D&C 88:7-13).

Investigators of the gospel are led by the Light of Christ. If men and women will hearken to the Spirit, it will lead them to the truths of the gospel and they will recognize them.

Lastly, the Holy Ghost works through the Light of Christ. The person of the Holy Ghost can work through the Spirit of Christ that permeates everything, or he can work by personal contact.[230]

By way of illustration, we will compare a light bulb in a lamp to Christ. The light bulb can only be in one place at a time. When the lamp is switched on, the light from the bulb radiates and fills a room. Christ can only be in one place at a time, but the Light of Christ proceeds forth from his presence and fills the immensity of space and is in all things.

OMNISCIENCE—ATTRIBUTE OF KNOWLEDGE AND TRUTH

Omniscience consists in having unlimited knowledge. In a revelation given to the Prophet Joseph Smith, January 2, 1831, we read these declarative words: "Thus saith the Lord your God, even Jesus Christ, the Great I am, Alpha and Omega, the beginning and the end, the same which looked upon the wide expanse of eternity, and all the seraphic [angelic] hosts of heaven, before the world was made;

"*The same which knoweth all things,* for all things are present before mine eyes . . ." (D&C 38:1-2) (See also 2 Ne. 9:20; D&C 88:7-13).

We are further informed that God—which includes both the Father and the Son—has "all power, all wisdom, and all understanding" (Alma 26:35). In addition, he possesses *"a fulness of truth, yea, even of all truth"* (D&C 93:11, 26).

In speaking of the attributes of God, the Prophet Joseph

Smith said: "Seeing that without the knowledge of all things God would not be able to save any portion of his creatures . . . *and if it were not for the idea existing in the minds of men that God had all knowledge it would be impossible for them to exercise faith in him.*" [231]

Elder McConkie has provided this important insight: "God has all power; he is the Almighty. He knows all things, and there is nothing in all eternity, in universe upon universe, that he does not know. Joseph Smith so taught, and all our scriptures, ancient and modern, bear a concordant testimony. *He is not a student God, and he is not progressing in knowledge or learning new truths.* If he knows how to create and govern worlds without number, and all that on them is, what is there left for him to learn?" [232]

Though these statements aptly prove that God has all knowledge, there are those individuals who still hold to the thought that God is progressing in knowledge. Regarding this type of false thinking, we turn to the expressions of Elder Joseph Fielding Smith.

"It seems very strange to me that members of the Church will hold to the doctrine, 'God increases in knowledge as time goes on.' Or that they can believe (as a recently published article says): 'If absolute perfection were attainable, there would eventually come a time when those who had chosen the better way would reach the ultimate; and if the ultimate could be gained, progression would cease . . .'"

Elder Smith then asks: "Where has the Lord ever revealed to us that he is lacking in knowledge? That he is still learning new truth; discovering new laws that are unknown to him?" He then gives his thoughts on the subject: "*I think this kind of doctrine is very dangerous.* I don't know where the Lord has ever declared such a thing. It is not contained in any revelation that I have read. Man's *opinion unaided by the revelations of the Lord, does not make it so.*" [233]

With this understanding, we turn to the expression of Hyrum Smith, Patriarch to the Church. He simply but powerfully stated: *"I would not* serve a God that had not all wisdom and all power." [234]

Concerning this statement, Elder Joseph Fielding Smith expressed these thoughts: "Do we believe that God has all *'wisdom'*? If so, in that, he is absolute. If there is something he does not know, then he is not absolute in 'wisdom,' and to think such a thing is absurd. Does he have all *'power'*? If so then there is nothing in which he lacks. If he is lacking in 'wisdom' and in 'power' then he is not supreme and there must be something greater than he is, and this is absurd." [235]

Thus, we have several statements by the Lord's chosen servants informing us that God has all knowledge, all wisdom, and all power. The Father and the Son are truly omniscient Gods.

18

THE FULNESS OF THE FATHER—GOD'S SON DID NOT RECEIVE A FULNESS AT FIRST

King Benjamin said that "the Lord Omnipotent" would come to earth and dwell among the children of men with a physical body. Giving further explanation, this righteous man said that "he shall be called Jesus Christ, the Son of God . . . the Creator of all things from the beginning; and his mother shall be called Mary . . ." (Mosiah 3:2, 5, 8).

Though the premortal Lord was a member of the Godhood, and had great authority and power, he had to come to earth and first obtain a mortal body; secondly a resurrected, immortal body, before he could enter into the fulness of the glory of his Father and his God. While on this earth, Jesus had to work out his own salvation by doing the will of his Father in all things. As the Apostle Paul has aptly explained, "Though he were a Son, yet learned he obedience by the things which he suffered (Heb. 5:8). By overcoming the sins and temptations of the world, the mortal Jesus Christ was "being made perfect" (Heb. 5:9).

It was John, whom many call the Baptist, who has written these informative words concerning the mortal progression and achievement of our Lord and Savior. "And I, John, saw that he received not of the fulness at first . . . but continued from grace to grace, until he received a fulness; And thus he was called the Son of God, because he received not of the fulness at the first." Then, after telling of the baptism of our Lord, he declares: "And I, John, bear record that he received a fulness of the glory of the Father; And he received all power, both in heaven and on earth, and the glory of the Father was with him, for he dwelt in him" (D&C 93:12-17). This declaration is supported by what the resurrected Lord said to eleven of the New Testament apostles: "All power is given unto me in heaven and in earth" (Matt. 28:16, 18).

ATTRIBUTES OF GODLINESS IN THEIR FULNESS

In their fulness and perfection, both the Father and the Son possess all godly attributes. To name a few: They possess all charity—which "is the pure love of Christ" (Moroni 7:47). Meaning: "It is love so centered in righteousness that the possessor has no aim or desire except for the eternal welfare of his own soul and for the souls of those around him (2 Ne. 26:30; Moroni 7:47; 8:25-26).[236]

The Father and Son possess all *love*. John wrote: ". . . God is love; and he that dwelleth in love dwelleth in God, and God in him" (1 John 4:16). Further: ". . . If we love one another, God dwelleth in us, and his love is perfected in us" (1 John 4:12). Therefore, the highest manifestation of love on man's part is his devotion to God; then, his attitude and kindness toward mankind.

The Father and Son possess all *mercy*. Paraphrasing what the Prophet Joseph Smith said, mercy is an attribute of Deity; therefore, mankind is able to have faith in Deity unto life and salvation. That God will have compassion for them in all their afflictions and tribulations (*Lectures on Faith*, pp. 46-47).

Likewise, the atoning sacrifice of our Lord came about because of his infinite mercy (D&C 29:1). Though the Father and Son have all mercy, we are told "that mercy hath no claim" on any man or woman unless he or she repents and turns to the Lord (Mosiah 2:38-39). We are further informed that "mercy hath compassion on mercy and claimeth her own; justice continueth its course and claimeth its own . . ." (D&C 88:40). Justice is demanded of all those who have committed sin and do not repent. However, "If ye will repent, and harden not your hearts," saith God, "then will I have mercy upon you, through mine Only Begotten Son; Therefore, whosoever repenteth, and hardened not his heart, he shall have claim on mercy through mine Only Begotten Son, unto a remission of his sins; and these shall enter into my rest" (Alma 12:33-34). From these teachings, we learn that mercy cannot rob justice. However, mercy is applied in full measure for those who love and serve God and repent of their sins.

The Father and Son are also the possessors of all *truth* (D&C 93:24), all *wisdom*, (Alma 26:35; D&C 76:2), and all *power* (Matt.28:18; D&C 93:17). Thus, individually and collectively, the Father and the Son are the personification and embodiment of all godly attributes.

By our faithfulness, we, too, can become like the Father and his Son. By becoming a god, we also will obtain all godly attributes in their fulness.

WHAT IS THE FULNESS OF GOD?

Elder McConkie has written these words: "Paul said to his Ephesian brethren: I pray to the Father that you shall 'be strengthen with might by his Spirit in the inner man; That Christ may dwell in your hearts by faith,' until through knowledge, obedience, and righteousness 'ye might be filled with all the fulness of God' (Eph.3:14-19).

"'The fulness of God'! What is it?" asks our apostolic scholar. Answering his own question, he simply says: *"It is to be one with the Father."* Then, he gives this explanation: "Jesus spoke of gaining 'all power . . . in heaven and in earth' (Matt. 28:18). Such is the reward for all those who 'pass by the angels, and the gods, . . . to their exaltation and glory in all things . . . which glory shall be a fulness . . . Then shall they be gods'" (D&C 132:19-20).[237]

From another of his works, we obtain this additional information: "To gain the *fulness of the Father* means to attain exaltation and godhood. *This fulness consists of (1) all power, both in heaven and on earth, and (2) eternal increase or a 'continuation of the seeds forever and ever'" (D&C 132:19:24).*[238]

The plan of salvation, for mankind in this life, is the gospel of Jesus Christ. It comprises all of the laws, ordinances, and performances that are necessary for our Father's children to gain eternal life. From what has been revealed by the Prophet Joseph Smith and the teachings from the four Standard Works of the Church, we are correctly taught that the Father's plan of Salvation is an eternal plan; the same identical plan that allowed our Father to gain exaltation and become our Heavenly Father.

We further know that our Father in Heaven is not a single Parent; he is married and lives in an eternal family unit. We have a Mother in Heaven. Not only did our Father in Heaven and his Eternal Companion gain eternal life, they have also gained *eternal lives*. In addition to living forever as an exalted Husband and Wife, they are able to have an eternal increase, a continuation of the seeds forever. Thus, all of mankind on this earth is the spirit children of our Heavenly Parents!

THE PLAN OF EXALTATION

The plan of exaltation, which personifies the eternal plan of salvation, is one whereby those who are faithful to all of the

THE ETERNAL FATHER AND HIS SON

laws and ordinances of the gospel can gain the fulness of the Father. From the revealed word, we learn that obedience to the whole law of the gospel of Jesus Christ, including the crowning ordinance of celestial marriage, is the only way whereby the fulness of the Father can be obtained. Those so married, and the marriage is "sealed unto them by the Holy Spirit of promise, by him who is anointed," and they remain faithful to the end, shall go on "to their exaltation and glory in all things . . . which glory shall be a fulness and a continuation of the seeds forever and ever. Then shall they be gods . . . because they have all power, and the angels are subject unto them" (D&C 132:6, 19-20).

In harmony with this teaching, the Prophet Joseph Smith taught: ". . . and all those who keep his [the Father's] commandments shall grow up from grace to grace, and become heirs of the heavenly kingdom, and joint-heirs with Jesus Christ; possessing the same mind, being transformed into the same image or likeness . . . being filled with the *fullness of his glory, and become one in him*, even as the Father [and] Son . . . are one."

Later, he writes: "As the Son partakes of the fullness of the Father through the Spirit, *so the saints are, by the same Spirit, to be partakers of the same fullness, and enjoy the same glory . . .*"[239]

From what is written in the revelations, we are informed that if we are faithful to the end of our mortal lives to the saving laws and ordinances of the gospel, we shall receive a fullness of the Father and a continuation of the seeds forever.

"Exaltation consists of an inheritance in the highest heaven of the celestial world," says Elder McConkie, "where alone the family unit continues and where each recipient gains for himself an eternal family unit, patterned after the family of God our Heavenly Father, so that every exalted person lives the kind of life which God lives and is therefore one with him."[240]

OUR GLORIOUS GOAL

From all that has been presented in this work, we know that the Father and the Son are glorified, exalted beings with tangible bodies of flesh and bones (D&C 130:22). From inspired teachings, we are correctly taught that the gospel of Jesus Christ is our Father's eternal plan of salvation. We are further informed that God is the Father and God of all mankind, Christ included.

We further know that the Father is not a single Parent; that he lives in an eternal family unit. By reason that God is our Heavenly Father, his work and glory is to bring to pass the immortality and eternal life of man (Moses 1:39).

By obedience to the whole law of the gospel of Jesus Christ, and enduring in righteousness to the end of our mortal lives, we can become a god. As has been discussed, we know that by obedience to all the laws and ordinances of the gospel, including the crowning ordinance of celestial marriage, we can be exalted. Thereby, we can receive a fulness of the Father and a continuation of the seeds forever. Therefore, our glorious goal is to become like the Eternal Father and his Son; being partakers of the same fulness, and enjoying the same glory!

CHAPTER NOTES

Chapter One

1. *Doctrines of Salvation*, Sermons and Writings of Joseph Fielding Smith, compiled by Bruce R. McConkie, Vol. 1, Bookcraft, 1954, p. 2; Presbyterian Confession of Faith, chapter 2.

2. James E. Talmage, *The Articles of Faith*, April, 1899, Twelfth Edition, 1924, pp. 47-48.

3. Milton R. Hunter, *The Gospel Through the Ages*, Deseret Book, 1958, p. 91.

4. President George Q. Cannon, *Journal of Discourses*, Vol. 24, p. 372.

5. President Brigham Young, *Journal of Discourses*, Vol. 16, p. 31.

6. Orson Pratt, *Millennial Star* 11: 238, August 1, 1849.

7. President Heber J. Grant, An Address to Seminary Teachers, delivered July 13, 1934, *Teach That Which Encourages Faith*, pp. 14-15 (From a 20-page pamphlet).

8. Joseph Fielding Smith, *The Improvement Era* 38: pp. 208-209, April, 1935.

Chapter Two

9. *Documentary History of the Church*, Vol. 4, p. 535.

10. President Gordon B. Hinckley, First Counselor to President Ezra Taft Benson, a pamphlet titled, *The Father, Son, & Holy Ghost*, Bookcraft, 1988, p. 3.

11. President Charles W. Penrose, *Conference Report*, April 3, 1921, pp. 13-14.

12. Bruce R. McConkie, *A New Witness for the Articles of Faith*, Deseret Book, 1985, p. 58.

13. Bruce R. McConkie, *Doctrinal New Testament Commentary*, Vol. 1, The Gospels, Bookcraft, 1965, p. 124.

14. Joseph Fielding Smith, *Teachings of the Prophet Joseph Smith*, 1938, p. 190.

15. *Doctrines of Salvation*, "Sermons and Writings of Joseph Fielding Smith:" compiled by Bruce R. McConkie, Vol. 1, Bookcraft, 1954, p. 74; Bruce R. McConkie, *A New Witness for the Articles of Faith*, Deseret Book Company, 1985, p. 63.

16. *Doctrines of Salvation*, "Sermons and Writings of Joseph Fielding Smith", compiled by Bruce R. McConkie, Vol. 1, Bookcraft, 1954, p. 27.

17. Bruce R. McConkie, *Doctrinal New Testament Commentary*, Vol. 1, The Gospels, Bookcraft, 1965, p. 468.

18. Bruce R. McConkie, *A New Witness for the Articles of Faith*, Deseret Book Company, 1985, p. 63.

19. Ibid., p. 63.

20. Ibid., p. 51.

21. B.H. Roberts, First Council of Seventy, An Address, May 20, 1914, *Deseret News Semi-Weekly*, No. 38, p. 9, July 2, 1914.

Chapter Three

22. Joseph Fielding Smith, *Teachings of the Prophet Joseph Smith*, 1938, p. 342.

23. D&C 21; Joseph Fielding Smith, *Essentials in Church History*, pp. 91-92; *Documentary History of the Church*, Vol. 1, pp. 60-61; 75-78; See also the author's book, *Glad Tidings Near Cumorah*, Cedar Fort, 2004, pp. 18, 117.

24. Joseph Fielding Smith, *Essentials in Church History*, p. 353.

25. Joseph Fielding Smith, *Teachings of the Prophet Joseph Smith*, 1938, pp. 343-345.

26. Joseph Smith—History 1: 14-20; *Documentary History of the Church*, Vol. 1, pp. 5-6; Vol. 4, *The Wentworth Letter*, p. 536; See also the author's book, *Glad Tidings Near Cumorah*, Cedar Fort, 2004, pp. 20-30.

27. Joseph Fielding Smith, *Teachings of the Prophet Joseph Smith*, pp. 345-346.

28. *Gospel Doctrine*, Selections from The Sermons and Writings of Joseph F. Smith, Sixth President of The Church of Jesus Christ of Latter-day Saints, Eighteenth Printing, Deseret Book, 1973, p. 32.

29. *Discourses of Brigham Young*, Selected and Arranged by John A. Widtsoe, 1973 edition, p. 22.

30. Joseph Fielding Smith, *Teachings of the Prophet Joseph Smith*, 1938, p. 354.

31. *Gospel Doctrine*, p. 11.

32. President George Q. Cannon, *Journal of Discourses*, Vol. 26, p. 79.

33. Hyrum L. Andrus, *Doctrinal Commentary on the Pearl of Great Price*, Deseret Book Company, 1967, pp. 497-498.

34. *Teachings of the Prophet Joseph Smith*, p. 373.

35. Ibid., p. 373.

36. Ibid., p. 373.

37. *Discourses of Brigham Young*, p. 22.

38. Luke 3: 38; Moses 6: 22; Elder Bruce R. McConkie, *Mormon Doctrine*, 2nd ed., p. 742; see also the author's book, *Mysteries of the Kingdom*, pp. 13-19.

39. *Discourses of Brigham Young*, p. 22.

40. Bishop Orson F. Whitney, *Journal of Discourses*, Vol. 26, pp. 196-197.

41. Hyrum Andrus, *Doctrinal Commentary on the Pearl of Great Price*, Deseret Book Company, 1967, pp. 497-498.

Chapter Four

42. Bruce R. McConkie, *The Promised Messiah, The first coming of Christ*, Deseret Book Company, 1978, pp. 139-140.

43. Bruce R. McConkie, *Mormon Doctrine*, 2nd ed., Bookcraft, 1966, p. 467.

44. Ibid., p. 655.

45. Orson Pratt, *Journal of Discourses*, Vol. 2, p. 342.

46. Bruce R. McConkie, *Mormon Doctrine*, 2nd ed., Bookcraft, 1966, p. 29.

47. Ibid., p. 30.

48. Bruce R. McConkie, *A New Witness for the Articles of Faith*, Deseret Book Company, 1985, p. 63.

49. James E. Talmage, *Jesus The Christ*, 1962 ed., p. 38.

50. Bruce R. McConkie, *Mormon Doctrine*, 2nd. ed., Bookcraft, 1966, p. 224.

51. Ibid., p. 226.

52. Ibid., p. 233.

53. Ibid., p. 278.

54. Ibid., p. 317.

55. *Lectures on Faith*, p. 9.

56. Bruce R. McConkie, *Mormon Doctrine*, 2nd ed., Bookcraft, 1966, p. 318.

57. Ibid., p. 355.

58. Ibid., pp. 544-545.

59. Ibid., p. 450.

60. Ibid., p. 451.

61. Ibid., p. 516.

62. Brigham Young, *Journal of Discourses*, Volume 1, page 50

Chapter Five

63. President Brigham Young, a discourse given at the Salt Lake City Tabernacle, February 8, 1857; as recorded in the *Journal of Discourses*, Vol. 4, pp. 215-216.

64. Ibid., p. 218.

65. President Brigham Young, a discourse given in the Salt Lake City Tabernacle, October 6, 1859; as recorded in the *Journal of Discourses*, Vol. 7, pp. 274-275.

66. Orson F. Whitney, *Journal of Discourses*, Vol. 26, p. 194.

67. Ibid., pp. 195-197.

68. Ibid., p. 194.

69. Orson Pratt, *The Seer*, October, 1853, Vol. 1, pp. 158-159.

70. Erastus Snow, a discourse in the Provo Tabernacle, Sunday, May

THE ETERNAL FATHER AND HIS SON

31, 1885; as recorded in *Journal of Discourses*, Vol. 26, p. 214.

71. Bruce R. McConkie, *Mormon Doctrine*, 2nd ed., Bookcraft, 1966, p. 516.

72. Ibid., pp. 516-517.

73. Ibid., p. 517.

74. Ibid., p. 238.

Chapter Six

75. President Brigham Young, A discourse given in Farmington, Utah, August 24, 1872; as recorded in *Journal of Discourses*, Vol. 15, p. 137.

76. Statement by First Presidency, printed in *The Improvement Era*, 13: 80; November 1909.

77. *Man: His Origin and Destiny*, by Joseph Fielding Smith, Deseret Book Company, 1954, p. 344. Also found in Messages of the First Presidency, Vol. 4, p. 266.

78. *Teachings of the Prophet Joseph Smith*, p. 373.

79. President Joseph F. Smith, An address, December 7, 1913, *Deseret Evening News*, December 27, 1913, p. 7; also quoted in *Church News Section*, September 19, 1936, pp. 2, 8.

80. *Course of study for Priests*—1910. Prepared and issued under the direction of the General Authorities of the Church; December 4, 1909. The General Committee consists of Rudger Clawson, David O. McKay, Seymour B. Young, B. H. Roberts, Rulon S. Wells, Joseph W. McMurrin, Charles W. Nibley, etc.; p. 37.

81. Statement by First Presidency, printed in *The Improvement Era*, 13: 80; November 1909.

82. Bruce R. McConkie, *Mormon Doctrine*, 2nd ed., Bookcraft, 1966, p. 742.

83. Bruce R. McConkie, *The Promised Messiah: The first coming of Christ*, Deseret Book Company, 1978, p. 597.

Chapter Seven

84. The reader is informed that most of the information in this chapter is taken from the author's book, *Mary, Mother of Jesus*, Cedar Fort, 2001.

85. Bruce R. McConkie, *The Mortal Messiah: From Bethlehem to Calvary*, Book 1, Note 4, Deseret Book Company, 1979. pp. 326-327.

86. Bruce R. McConkie, Council of the Twelve, an address, June 29, 1978, at the dedication Services at Nauvoo, pp. 3-5; ("Source of Quote") Copyright: The Church of Jesus Christ of Latter-day Saints. Used by permission.

87. *Teachings of the Prophet Joseph Smith*, 1938, p. 157.

88. James E. Talmage, *Jesus The Christ*, 1962, p. 80.

89. Bruce R. McConkie, *The Mortal Messiah: From Bethlehem to Calvary*, Book 1, Deseret Book Company, 1979, pp. 413-414.

Chapter Eight

90. James E. Talmage, *Jesus the Christ*, 1962 ed., p. 81.

91. The reader is informed that most of the information in this chapter is taken from the author's book, *Mary, Mother of Jesus*, Cedar Fort, 2001.

92. Heber C. Kimball, *Journal of Discourses*, Vol. 8, p. 211; September 2, 1860.

93. Brigham Young, *Journal of Discourses*, Vol. 8, p. 115.

94. Bruce R. McConkie, *Mormon Doctrine*, 2nd ed., Bookcraft, 1966, p. 547.

95. Ibid., p. 742.

96. Bruce R. McConkie, *Doctrinal New Testament Commentary*, Vol. 1, The Gospels, Bookcraft, 1965. Bookcraft, pp. 82-83.

97. Ibid., p. 82.

98. Bryant S. Hinckley, *Sermons and Missionary Services of Melvin Joseph Ballard*, Deseret Book Company, 1949, pp. 166-167.

99. Orson Pratt, Council of the Twelve, *The Seer*, Washington D.C. Edition, October, 1853, p. 158.

100. Ibid., November, 1853, p. 172.

101. President Brigham Young, *Journal of Discourses*, Vol. 11, p. 268; August 19, 1866.

THE ETERNAL FATHER AND HIS SON

102. President Joseph F. Smith, an address given at Box Elder Stake Conference, December 20, 1914; printed in the *Box Elder News* of January 18, 1915.

103. Bryant S. Hinckley, *Sermons and Missionary Services of Melvin Joseph Ballard*, Deseret Book Company, 1949, p. 166.

Chapter Nine

104. Bruce R. McConkie, *The Mortal Messiah: From Bethlehem to Calvary*, Book 1, Deseret Book, 1979, p. 344.

105. Ibid., p. 369-370.

106. Ibid., p. 374.

107. Ibid., p. 377.

108. James E. Talmage, *Jesus the Christ*, 1962, p. 113.

109. Bruce R. McConkie, *The Mortal Messiah: From Bethlehem to Calvary*, Book 1, Deseret Book Company, 1979, p. 369.

110. Ibid., p. 408.

111. Bruce R. McConkie, *A New Witness for the Articles of Faith*, Deseret Book Company, 1985, pp. 191-192.

112. Ibid., p. 199.

113. Sheri L. Dew, *Go Forward With Faith*, the biography of Gordon B. Hinckley, Deseret Book Company, 1996, p. 84.

114. Bruce R. McConkie, *Doctrinal New Testament Commentary*, Vol. 1, The Gospels, Bookcraft, Third Printing, 1972, p. 192.

115. Bruce R. McConkie, *The Mortal Messiah: From Bethlehem to Calvary*, Book 1, Deseret Book Company, 1979, p. 369.

116. Bruce R. McConkie, *Doctrinal New Testament Commentary*, Vol. 1, The Gospels, Bookcraft, Third Printing, 1972, p. 191.

Chapter Ten

117. Bruce R. McConkie, *Mormon Doctrine*, 2nd ed., Bookcraft, 1966, p. 387.

118. Ibid., p. 164.

119. James E. Talmage, *Jesus the Christ*, 1962 ed., p. 126.

120. Ibid., pp. 126-127.

121. Bruce R. McConkie, *Doctrinal New Testament Commentary*, Vol. 1, The Gospels, Bookcraft, 1972, p. 124.

122. Bruce R. McConkie, *The Mortal Messiah, From Bethlehem to Calvary*, Book 1, Deseret Book Company, 1979, p. 401.

123. James E. Talmage, *Jesus the Christ*, 1962 ed., p. 376. See also the author's book, Simon Peter, Cedar Fort, 2002, pp. 148-149.

124. Ibid., p. 370.

125. Joseph Fielding Smith, *Teachings of the Prophet Joseph Smith*, 1938, p. 158.

126. *Doctrines of Salvation*, Vol. 2, p. 107-111; *Teachings of the Prophet Joseph Smith*, pp. 172, 323, 330-335.

127. Bruce R. McConkie, *Doctrinal New Testament Commentary*, Vol. 1, *The Gospels*, Bookcraft, 1972, p. 403.

128. Ibid., p. 61.

129. Dr. Sidney B. Sperry, *The Book of Mormon Testifies*, Bookcraft, Fourth Edition, 1960, p. 294. Used by permission.

130. Ibid., p. 294. Used by permission.

131. Bruce R. McConkie, *The Mortal Messiah: From Bethlehem to Calvary*, Book 4, Deseret Book Company, 1985, pp. 306-307. Used by permission.

132. George Q. Cannon, *The Life of Joseph Smith*, first edition, 1888, pp. 36-37.

133. Bruce R. McConkie, *A New Witness for the Articles of Faith*, Deseret Book Company, 1985, p. 6.

134. *Doctrines of Salvation*, Sermons and Writings of Joseph Fielding Smith, compiled by Bruce R. McConkie, Vol. 1, Bookcraft, 1954, p. 27.

Chapter Eleven

135. James E. Talmage, *Jesus the Christ*, 1962 ed., p. 400.

136. Bruce R. McConkie, *The Mortal Messiah: From Bethlehem to Calvary*, Book 3, Deseret Book Company, 1980, p. 125.

137. Bishop Orson F. Whitney, *Journal of Discourses*, Vol. 26, pp. 196-197.

138. James E. Talmadge, *Jesus the Christ*, 1962 ed. p.400.

139. Ibid., p. 400.

140. Bruce R. McConkie, *Doctrinal New Testament Commentary*, Vol. 1, *The Gospels*, Bookcraft, 1972, pp. 441-442.

141. Ibid., p. 157.

142. For a further discussion on the marriage in Cana of Galilee, refer to the author's book, *Mary, Mother of Jesus*, Cedar Fort, 2001, pp. 133-136.

143. Bruce R. McConkie, *Doctrinal New Testament Commentary*, Vol. 1, *The Gospels*, Bookcraft, 1972, pp. 441-442.

144. Ibid., p. 153.

145. Bruce R. McConkie, *The Mortal Messiah: From Bethlehem to Calvary*, Book 3, Deseret Book Company, 1980, p. 419.

Chapter Twelve

146. Bruce R. McConkie, *The Promised Messiah: The first coming of Christ*, Deseret Book Company, 1978, p. 597.

147. Some of the information is taken from the author's book, *The Three Nephites and Other Translated Beings*, Cedar Fort, 2003, pp. 69-70.

148. Ibid., p. 599.

149. Bruce R. McConkie, *The Millennial Messiah*, Deseret Book Company, 1982, p. 644. For a more thorough study on translated beings, the reader is referred to the author's book, *The Three Nephites and other Translated Beings*, Cedar Fort, 2003.

150. Bruce R. McConkie, *A New Witness for the Articles of Faith*, Deseret Book Company, 1985, p. 495.

151. Joseph Fielding Smith, *Essentials in Church History*, pp. 188; *Documentary History of the Church*, Vol. 2, p. 379.

152. *Documentary History of the Church*, Vol. 2, pp. 380-381.

153. *Documentary History of the Church*, Vol. 1, p. 84.

154. Ibid., p. 85.

155. Ibid., p. 176, Notes.

156. Ibid., Vol. 1, p. 322-323.

157. Salt Lake School of Prophets, 1883 Minute Book, pp. 37-39, October 3, 1883. Concerning the Salt Lake School of Prophets, see Elder Bruce R. McConkie, *Mormon Doctrine*, 2nd ed. Bookcraft, 1966, p.681.

158. Alfred Douglas Young, Autobiographical Journal, 1808-1842, pp. 3-13.

Chapter Thirteen

159. Bruce R. McConkie, *The Promised Messiah: The first coming of Christ*, Deseret Book Company, 1978, p. 599.

160. For a more thorough study on Moses as a translated being, see the author's book, *The Three Nephites and Other Translated Beings*, Cedar Fort, 2003, pp. 79-82.

161. *Juvenile Instructor*, Vol. 27, p. 282; *The Improvement Era*, Vol. 8, pp. 704-705. See also Elder Bruce R. McConkie, *Mormon Doctrine*, 2nd ed., p. 463.

Chapter Fourteen

162. Concerning this date, the reader is referred to the author's book, *Simon Peter*, Cedar Fort, 2002, pp. 217.

163. James E. Talmage, *Jesus the Christ*, 1962 ed., p. 681.

164. Ibid., p. 265. For a reason why Jesus appeared to Mary, reference the author's book, *Mysteries of the Kingdom*, Cedar Fort, 2001, pp. 33-41.

165. To support the claim that she is the sister of Jesus' mother, Mary, reference the author's book, *Mary, Mother of Jesus*, Cedar Fort, 2001, pp. 21-23.

166. Bruce R. McConkie, *The Mortal Messiah: From Bethlehem to Calvary*, Book 4, Deseret Book Company, p. 265.

167. Ibid., p. 267.

168. Ibid., pp. 267.

THE ETERNAL FATHER AND HIS SON

169. Information partially taken from the author's book, *Simon Peter*, Cedar Fort, 2002.

170. Bruce R. McConkie, *The Mortal Messiah: From Bethlehem to Calvary*, Book 4, Deseret Book Company, p. 296.

171. Ibid., p. 711.

172. Ibid., p. 712.

173. Ibid., p. 714.

174. Ibid., p. 715.

175. For a more thorough study of John as a translated being, reference the author's book, *The Three Nephites and Other Translated Beings*, Cedar Fort, 2003, pp. 83-86.

176. James E. Talmage, *Jesus the Christ*, 1962 ed., p. 717.

177. For a more thorough study, reference the author's book, *The Three Nephites and Other Translated Beings*, Cedar Fort, 2003, pp. 1-47.

178. Bruce R. McConkie, *The Mortal Messiah: From Bethlehem to Calvary*, Book 4, Deseret Book Company, p. 252.

179. Ibid., p. 253.

Chapter Fifteen

180. *Documentary History of the Church*, Vol. 1, p. 84.

181. Ibid., p. 85.

182. Ibid., p. 176, Notes.

183. Diary of Mary Elisabeth Rollins Lightner, unpublished manuscript, pp. 2-4.

184. *The Utah Genealogical And Historical Magazine*, Vol. XXVIII, No. 2, p. 61; April, 1937.

185. *Documentary History of the Church*, Vol. 1, pp. 242-243, 245; D&C 75; Joseph Fielding Smith, *Essentials in Church History*, 19th Edition, 1964, pp. 143-144.

186. Joseph Fielding Smith, *Essentials in Church History*, pp. 188; *Documentary History of the Church*, Vol. 2, p. 379.

187. Joseph Fielding Smith, *Essentials in Church History*, pp. 188; *Documentary History of the Church*, Vol. 2, pp. 379-380.

188. *Documentary History of the Church*, Vol. 2, pp. 378-380.

189. Ibid., pp. 381-382.

190. Ibid., Vol. 1, p. 322-323.

191. Salt Lake School of Prophets, 1883 Minute Book, pp. 37-39; October 3, 1883. Concerning the Salt Lake School of Prophets, see Elder Bruce R. McConkie, *Mormon Doctrine*, 2nd ed., Bookcraft, 1966, p.681.

192. *Documentary History of the Church*, Vol. 2, pp. 386-387.

193. George A. Smith, An Address in the Tabernacle, Ogden City, on Tuesday, November 15, 1864, as recorded in *Journal of Discourses*, Vol. 11, p. 10.

194. Ibid., pp. 410-428.

195. Ibid., p. 434-435.

196. The Revised Edition of the *Doctrine and Covenants Commentary*, as printed by Deseret Book Company, 1951, with comments by The Publication Committee—Elders Joseph Fielding Smith, Harold B. Lee, Marion G. Romney. Paraphrased words taken from pg.s 723-724.

197. *Documentary History of the Church*, Vol. 2, pp. 434-435.

198. Ibid., p. 435.

199. *Documentary History of the Church*, Vol. 2, pp. 430-433; Joseph Fielding Smith, *Essentials in Church History*, p. 190.

200. Alfred Douglas Young, *Autobiographical Journal*, 1808-1842, pp. 3-13.

201. *The Relief Society Magazine* 9:141, March, 1922. *The Utah Genealogical And Historical Magazine* 5:62, April, 1914.

202. Kenneth G. Godfrey, *A History Of The Church 1891-1897*, A Paper presented to The Department of Graduate Studies in Religious Instruction, B.Y.U., Provo, Utah, April, 1955, p. 5.

203. Erastus Beaman Snow, *Erastus Beaman Snow Journal*, April 20, 1893, LDS Church Archives, Ms f 134 #1, Ms d 4013, Bx 1, fd. 5.

204. President George Q. Cannon, of the First Presidency, An Address, October 6, 1896, as printed in *Deseret News Weekly*, 53: 610-611, No. 20, October 31, 1896.

205. John Lee Johns, *Biography of John Lee Jones*, April 1893, Brigham Young University Special Collections—Mor M270.1 J714.

206. LeRoi C. Snow, "An Experience of My Father's," *The Improvement Era* 36: 677, 679, September, 1933. Other references: *Deseret News*, Church Section, April 2, 1938, p. 8; *Revelation*, by Lewis J. Harmer, 1957, pp. 118-121; *The Ensign* magazine, August 1975, pp. 19-20.

Chapter Sixteen

207. Melvin J. Ballard, An Address, June 8, 1919, *The Improvement Era* 22:1032; *Conference Report*, October 7, 1917, pp. 111-12; Bryant S. Hinckley, *Sermons and Missionary Services of Melvin Joseph Ballard*, Deseret Book, 1949, p. 156; *The Faith of Our Pioneer Forefathers*, Bryant S. Hinckley, Salt Lake City: Deseret Book Company., 1956, pp. 226-227; Paul H. Dunn, *In Humility Our Savior*, Aspen Books, 1997, p. 93.

208. Melvin J. Ballard, *Conference Report*, April 4, 1920, pp. 40-41.

209. Rulon S. Wells, *Conference Report*, April 5, 1940, p. 41.

210. George F. Richards, *Conference Report*, October 6, 1946, p. 139; also in *Conference Report*, April 7, 1974, pp. 173-174; *The Ensign* magazine, May, 1974, p. 119.

211. LeGrand Richards, Brigham Young University Stake Conference Address, "The Greatest Of All God's Creations," Sunday, January 21, 1961, pp. 3-4.

212. Orson F. Whitney, An Address, October 5, 1889, *Millennial Star* 51: 739-740, November 25, 1889. See also *Millennial Star* 87:662-663, 666, for an address given June 7, 1925, in which Elder Whitney relates the same experience but in a slightly different way. The same for *Through Memory's Halls*, 1930, pp. 81-83; Also in *The Contributor* 16: 666-668, An Address, June 9, 1895; *The Improvement Era* 29:224-225, An Address, June 7, 1925; *Young Woman's Journal*, 36:470-475, An Address, June 7, 1925.

213. Gayla Wise, *The Sign Of The Son Of Man*, 1991, p. 79.

214. *Cherished Experiences*, compiled by Clare Middlemiss, Deseret Book Company, 1955, p. 102.

215. President David O. McKay, Second Counselor to President George Albert Smith, *Conference Report*, April 4, 1949, p. 182.

216. W. Cleon Skousen, *Treasures From The Book of Mormon*, Vol. 3, 1976, p. 3294.

217. Boyd K. Packer, *Teach Ye Diligently*, Deseret Book Company, 1975, p.71.

Chapter Seventeen

218. Bruce R. McConkie, *Mormon Doctrine*, 2nd. ed., Bookcraft, 1966, p. 452.

219. Ibid., p. 544.

220. B.H. Roberts, First Council of Seventy, *The Seventy's Course in Theology*, Fourth Year, 1911, pp. 67,70.

221. Orson Pratt, *Journal of Discourses*, Vol. 2, p. 343.

222. Orson F. Whitney, *Conference Report*, October 15, 1913, p. 98.

223. James E. Talmage, An Address, July 8, 1917, *Deseret News Semi-Weekly*, Number 46, p. 10, August 2, 1917.

224. Bruce R. McConkie, *Mormon Doctrine*, 2nd. ed., Bookcraft, 1966, p. 544.

225. Orson F. Whitney, *Conference Report*, October 15, 1913, p. 98.

226. B.H. Roberts, *The Nearness of God,* Delivered in the Salt Lake Tabernacle, Sunday, March 15, 1914 and quoted in: *Masterpieces of Latter-day Saint Leaders*, p. 45, by N.B. Lundwall.

227. Bruce R. McConkie, *The Truth About God*, Missionary Pamphlet, p. 16.

228. B. H. Roberts, *The Seventy's Course in Theology*, Fifth Year, *Divine Immanence and the Holy Ghost*, Yearbook 5: 8-10, *The Deseret News*, Salt Lake City, 1912.

229. *Doctrines of Salvation, Sermons and Writings of Joseph Fielding Smith,* compiled by Bruce R. McConkie, Vol. 1, Bookcraft, 1954, p. 51.

230. Ibid., pp. 51-54.

231. *Lectures on Faith*, Number 11, p. 43.

THE ETERNAL FATHER AND HIS SON

232. Bruce R. McConkie, Brigham Young U.niversity Address, January 6, 1985. *The Mystery Of Godliness*, p. 6.

233. Joseph Fielding Smith, *Doctrines of Salvation*, Vol. 1, pp. 7-8.

234. Hyrum Smith, Patriarch to the Church, An Address, April 7, 1844, *Documentary History of the Church*, Vol. 6, p. 300.

235. Joseph Fielding Smith, *Doctrines of Salvation*, Vol. 1, p. 5.

Chapter Eighteen

236. Bruce R. McConkie, *Mormon Doctrine*, 2nd ed., Bookcraft, 1966, p. 121.

237. Bruce R. McConkie, *The Promised Messiah: The First coming of Christ*, Deseret Book Company, 1978, p. 124.

238. Bruce R. McConkie, *Doctrinal New Testament Commentary*, Vol. 1, *The Gospels*, Bookcraft, 1972, p.76.

239. *Lectures on Faith*, Numbers 2 and 3, p. 49.

240. Bruce R. McConkie, *The Promised Messiah: The First coming of Christ*, Deseret Book Company, 1978, p. 130.

INDEX

-A-

Ability of the Father and Son:
  Orson Pratt's teaching of, 6
Abraham's record:
  name-titles of Godhead members in, 12, 16;
  teaching of Kolob, 73; , tells what happened at Grand Council in Heaven, 73-75;
  saw the premortal Lord, 102-104
Adam:
  in the image of God, was created, 18;
  God walked and talked with, 18; first man was, 42; Eve is wife of, 42; meaning of name of, 43; First Presidency's teaching of, 44-46; born of woman was, 45; had a navel, 46, creation of, and Eve, 44-48; Eve and, were born immortal, 47; a body brother to Christ is, 48; Eve is a body sister to Christ and, 48; in the garden Eve and , saw the Father and Son, 93; after the fall Eve and, only heard the voice of God, 94; after the fall Eve and, were visited by angels, 94;
  at Adam-ondi-Ahman the premortal Lord appeared to, and others, 101
Adam-ondi-Aham:
  the premortal Lord appeared to Adam, Seth, Enos, Cainan, Mahalaleel, Jared, Enoch, Methuselah at, 101
Ahman:
  revelation on exalted name-title of the Father, 27

Alma:
  saw the premortal Lord, 110
Almighty God:
  exalted name-title of the Father and Son is, 28
Andrus, Hyrum: 21, 24
Apostle: when Joseph Smith became an, 7
Apostles: New Testament apostles saw the resurrected Lord, 117-119
Apostasy, Great:
  reason for, 2-3
Articles of Faith:
  Joseph Smith wrote the, 9
Athanasian Creed: 3

-B-

Ballard, Melvin J.: 59;
  saw the resurrected Lord, 137-138
Baptism:
  separate members of Godhead at our Lord's, 11;
  James E. Talmage's teaching of, of our Lord, 75-76;
  Bruce R. McConkie's teaching of, of our Lord, 76-77
Beloved Son:
  the Father introduces his, 5, 11;
  in the pre-mortal existence the Father introduced his, 73-75; at the baptism of Jesus the Father introduced his, 75-77;
  at the transfiguration of Jesus the Father introduced his, 77-79; at the appearance of Jesus to the Nephites the Father introduced his, 79-81;
  the Father introduced his, to Joseph Smith, 81-84
Bodily transported:
  Jesus, Ezekiel, Nephi, Mary, and the son

THE ETERNAL FATHER AND HIS SON

of Helaman, and Philip were, 54.
Boy-Jesus:
   instruction of, 66-67; teaching of J. Reuben Clark, Jr. of, 67-68;
   James E. Talmage's teaching of, at age twelve, 68-69
Brother of Jared:
   saw the premortal Lord, 107-109; Joseph Smith revealed name of, 107

-C-

Cainan:
   saw the premortal Lord, 101
Calvin, John: 4
Cannon, George Q.: 5, 20, 82-83;
   saw the resurrected Lord, 133
Carried away in the Spirit:
   Mary was, 54, others were, 54
Cephas: *see* Peter
Clark, J. Reuben, Jr.: 67-68
Cleopas: saw the resurrected Lord, 116-117
Coltrin, Zebedee:
   Saw the Father and Son, 98-99, 128-129; in 1836, saw the Savior, 129
Conception of the Son of God:
   teaching concerning, 56-63;
   Melvin J. Ballard's teaching of the, 59-60
Council in Heaven: *see* Grand Council in Heaven
Council of Nice: 2-3
Cowdery, Oliver:
   Joseph Smith and, saw the resurrected Lord in the Kirtland Temple, 129-130
Creative events:
   two, exclusively the Father's, 13-14
Creative process:
   Father delegated, to the Son and others, 13
Creator:
   God the first is the, 12-14, 16;
   exalted name-title of the Father and Son is, 28-29

- D -

Daniel:
   saw the premortal Lord, 107
Deity:
   oneness of, 10
Dispensation of the fulness of time:
   1820 was the year of the, 81
Divine investiture of authority:
   Jehovah spoke by, 13, 25
Divine patriarchal order:
   teaching of Hyrum Andrus on, 21, 24
Doctrine:
   Jesus taught his Father's, 85, 87
Dust:
   account of Abraham and Moses says that Adam was formed from the , of the ground, 44

- E -

Earth:
   only an account of our, was revealed to Moses, 13;
   as a mortal man God lived on an, 19
Elohim:
   exalted name-title of the Father is, 29,
   Brigham Young's teaching concerning, 36;
   Mary's child was begotten by, 56;
   on the transfiguration of Christ, introduced his beloved Son, 78
Emer:
   saw the premortal Lord, 109
Emerson, Ralph Waldo:

Heber J. Grant adopted
motto of, 72
Endless and Eternal:
  exalted name-title of Father
  and Son, 30
Enoch:
  and his people were
  translated, 94;
  saw the Father and Son, 94;
  at Adam-ondi-Ahman,
  saw the premortal Lord, 101
Enos:
  the premortal Lord appeared
  to, 101
Eternal Life:
  Orson F. Whitney's teaching
  of, 23, 38
Eternal Lives:
  the Eternal Father and His
  Eternal Companion gained,
  156;
  the Father and his Companion
  are able to have a continuation
  of the seeds, 156
Eternal Plan of Salvation: 20,
  Orson F. Whitney's teaching
  of, 23
Eternity:
  Plan of Salvation operates
  throughout, 21
Eve:
  wife of Adam is, 42;
  creation of, and Adam, 42-48;
  created in image of our
  Heavenly Mother, p. 43;
  Adam and , were born
  immortal, 47;
  Bruce R. McConkie's teaching
  of Mary and, 50
Everlasting gospel:
  Orson F. Whitney's teaching
  of, 23, 38
Exalted name-titles of the Father:
  25-34
Ezekiel:
  saw the premortal Lord, 107

- F -

Faith:
  Joseph Smith's teachings on
  how men exercise, 70-71;
  Christ had authority and , to
  perform miracles, 72;
  the Father has the fullness of,
  72;
  Christ had, like his Father, 72
Fall of Adam:
  all revelation before, came
  by Jehovah; 13,
  all revelation since, comes
  by Christ, 13
Family:
  basic unit of the Church
  is the, 41
Family unit:
  Our Heavenly Parents live in
  an eternal, 41;
  our goal is to live in an
  eternal, 41
Father:
  physical attributes of the,
  5-6,15;
  Son and, appeared to Joseph
  Smith, 5-6, 11;
  Creator of all things is the, 12;
  the, delegated to Son and
  others many creative acts, 12;
  above Son and Holy Ghost is,
  15;
  supreme member of Godhead
  is the, 15-16; the, and Son
  have a body of flesh and
  bones, 15;
  the, lived on an earth as a
  mortal, 18-19;
  the, is an exalted man, 19-20;
  God the Father also had a
  Heavenly, 21-22;
  work and glory of our
  Heavenly, 23;

THE ETERNAL FATHER AND HIS SON

exalted name-title of the
Son and, 31;
Brigham Young's teaching
of our Heavenly, 36-37;
Adam and Eve are physical
children of the, 42-48;
Mary held in her arms the
son of the Eternal, 54,
Christ was born of Mary
and the Eternal, 56;
relationship of Mary and the,
61-63;
birth of Christ was probably
witnessed by his, 65;
special relationship between
the Son and his, 66;
the Boy-Jesus knew his
biological, 69;
Jesus went in the wilderness
to be with God the, 70;
faith is exercised in its
fullness by the, 72;
the Son is introduced by
his, on various occasions,
73-84;
no man cometh unto the,
but by Jesus, 100;
the resurrected Lord said that
the, had sent him, 118;
we can become like the, 157-158

Feast of Tabernacles:
Jesus taught at the, 85-86;
Bruce R. McConkie's teaching
that Jesus taught the gospel
at the, 86

First:
God the, 12, 16

First Article of Faith:
Gordon B. Hinckley's
teaching of, 9-10

First Presidency:
teaching on Heavenly Father
and Mother by, 40;
teaching of creation of
Adam by, 44-46

First Vision:
year of, 1;
accounts of, 4-7, 18; 81-84
Heber J. Grant's teaching of, 7;
foundation of LDS Church is,
81;
George Q. Cannon's teaching
of, 82-83

Flesh and bones:
Father and Son have bodies
of, 15;
the Holy Ghost has not a
body of, 15

Fulness:
God's Son did not receive a
fulness at first, 153-154;
God's Son did receive a
fulness, 154
attributes of Godliness in
their, 154-155;
the, of God, 155-156;
by our faithfulness, we can
gain the, of the Father, 157

- G -

Gabriel:
Angel who appeared to Mary
was, 52;
Joseph Smith revealed that
Noah was, 51

God:
true concept of, 7-8;
meaning of one, 10;
Christ is, 15; Holy Ghost is, 15,
Father is, 15;
Joseph Smith taught, was once
a mortal man, 18-19;
as a mortal man, lived on
an earth, 19;
our, had a Heavenly Father, 22;
each member of Godhead is
a, 31,
exalted name-title of, 31-32;
the account of Abraham and
Moses tells that, from man

176

from dust of the ground, 44;
by our obedience we can
become a, 157
Godhead:
   sectarian teaching of, 1-2;
   three members comprise,
   10-11, 16;
   oneness of, 10-11;
   supreme presidency or, 11;
   specific roles within, 12
Gods:
   Paul's teaching of, 14-15;
   Brigham Young's teaching
   of number of, 22-23
Gospel:
   Bruce R. McConkie's teaching
   that Jesus taught the, at the
   Feast of Tabernacles, 86;
   Orson F. Whitney's teaching
   that it is the everlasting, the
   unchangeable way of eternal
   life, 23, 86;
   the elders of Israel teach the
   same, Jesus taught, 89,
   the plan of salvation is the,
   of Jesus Christ, 156
Grand Council in Heaven,
   teaching of, 73-75
Grant, Heber J.: 7, 72
Gravity:
   resurrected beings not
   limited by, 5-6

- H -

Harris, Martin:
   Joseph Smith and, saw
   the resurrected Lord,
   125-126
Heavenly Father:
   God the Father is our, 21-22;
   God the Father had a, 21-22;
   our, laid down his life as did
   Jesus Christ, 22;
   teaching of First Presidency
   that Adam is in likeness of our,
   43
Heavenly Mother:
   Orson F. Whitney's teaching
   of a, 38;
   Orson Pratt's teaching of a,
   38-39;
   Erastus Snow's teaching
   of a, 39;
   Bruce R. McConkie's teaching
   of a, 39-40;
   hymn of Eliza R. Snow about
   a, 40-41;
   Eve was created in the
   image of our, 43
Heavenly Parent:
   the Father is our, 35;
   Brigham Young's teaching of
   God is our, 35-36;
   Orson F. Whitney's teaching
   of God is our, 37;
   logic leads us that our
   Father is not a single, 38-40;
   the Father is a, 42;
   mankind is formed in the
   image of our, 43
Heavenly Parents:
   logic leads us to the fact we
   have, 38;
   becoming like our, 41
Highest:
   exalted name-title of the
   Father is, 32;
   the, physically overshadowed
   Mary, 52, 57
Hinckley, Gordon B.: 9-10
Holy Ghost:
   God is, 15;
   personage of spirit is the, 15;
   B. H. Roberts' teaching of, 16
Hunter, Milton R.: 4

- I -

Immanent God:
   exalted name-title of the
   Father and Son is, 32

THE ETERNAL FATHER AND HIS SON

Intelligences:
    Bruce R. McConkie's teaching of, 73
Intercessory Prayer: 14, 35
Isaac: saw the premortal Lord, 105
Isaiah: saw the premortal Lord, 106-107

- J -

Jacob:
    saw the premortal Lord, 105-106, 110
James:
    the Lord's brother, saw the resurrected Lord, 119-120
Jared:
    the premortal Lord appeared to, 101
Jehovah:
    before fall all revelation came by, 13
Jesus Christ:
    after fall all revelation comes by, 13;
    God is, 15; physical attribute of, 15;
    Son of God is, 5, 8, 10-12, 15, 21, 25-27, 29, 33-34, 42;
    a body brother to Adam and Eve is, 48; ,
    was naturally begotten, 57;
    was taught from on high, 65-72
Joanna:
    saw the resurrected Lord, 115
John the Baptist: our Lord was baptized by, 11, 75;
    preached the same gospel as Jesus, 88,
Jesus did not receive a fulness at first, 154;
    Jesus did receive a fulness, 154
John, the revelator:
    saw the resurrected Lord, 122
Joshua: saw the premortal Lord, 106

- K -

Keys:
    Peter, James, and John received, 78
Kimball, Heber C., 56
Knight, Newel: saw the Father and Son, 97, 124
Kolob, Abraham's teaching of, 73

- L -

Lamoni:
    saw the premortal Lord, 110
Lehi:
    saw the premortal Lord, 109-110
Light of Christ: 149-150
Lord:
    exalted name-title of the Father and Son is, 33;
    the Mediator between God and man is the, 100;
    Mary Magdalene was first to see the resurrected, 112-114;
    other women saw the resurrected, 114-115;
    many have seen the resurrected, 113-144
    (see chapters 14-16)
Lost Tribes of Israel:
    Bruce R. McConkie's teaching that the resurrected Lord appeared to the, 122
Lucifer:
    in Grand Council of Heaven was, 74; ,
    wanted to amend the Father's plan of salvation, 74

Luke:
    saw the resurrected Lord, 116-117
Luther, Martin: 4,

- M -

Mahalaleel:

the premortal Lord
appeared to, 101
Mahonri Moriancumer: *see* Brother
of Jared
Man:
the Father once was a
mortal, 18-19;
the Father is an exalted, 18
Man of Counsel: 26
Man of Holiness:
Christ is the Son of the, 25-26,
exalted name-title of the
Father is, 25-26, 39
Man of Righteousness: 27
Mary:
the mother of James and
Joses saw the resurrected
Lord, 114-115
Mary, Mother of Jesus:
teachings concerning, 49-52;
name of, revealed to holy
men of God, 50;
Bruce R. McConkie's teaching
of Eve and, 50; ,
was a virgin, 52-53, 59
Nephi's vision of, 54;
carried away in the Spirit
was, 54-55
Mary Magdalene:
was the first mortal to see
the resurrected Lord, 112-114;
James E. Talmage's teachings
of Mary hearing the voice
of the risen Lord, 114,
Bruce R. McConkie's teaching
of , being the first mortal
to see a resurrected person, 114
McConkie, Bruce R.:
10-11, 13-15, 25-33, 39-41,
47-50, 54, 57-59, 65-66, 67-77,
83, 87, 89-90, 92-94, 100,
114-116, 120, 122, 145, 148,
148-149, 151, 157
McKay, David O.:
saw the resurrected Lord,
142-143
Mediator:
the Lord is the, between God
and man, 100
Methodist preacher:
Joseph Smith related vision
to, 6;
comments by, 7
Methuselah:
saw the premortal Lord, 101
Moroni: saw the premortal
Lord, 110-111
Mortal Man:
Joseph Smith taught God
once was a, 18
Moses:
writings of in Pearl of Great
Price, 12-13; writings of,
tells what happened at Grand
Council in Heaven, 73-75;
saw the premortal Lord,
104-105
Most High:
exalted name-title of the
Father and Son, 33
Mount of Transfiguration:
what transpired on the, 77-79
Murdock, John:
saw the resurrected Lord, 126

- N -

Naturally Begotten:
Heber C. Kimball's teaching
of, 57;
Brigham Young's teaching
of, 57; Elder McConkie's
teaching of, 57
Nauvoo:
Joseph Smith preached
greatest sermon in, 17
1844 population of, 17-18
Navel:
Adam had a, 46
Neibaur, Alexander:
saw the resurrected Lord, 132

THE ETERNAL FATHER AND HIS SON

Nephi:
    vision of Mary by, 53-54;
    saw the premortal Lord, 109-110
Nephites:
    Sidney B. Sperry's teaching of Christ appearing to the, 79;
    Bruce R. McConkie's teaching of Christ appearing to the, 80;
    resurrected Lord appeared to, 122
Noah: *See* Gabriel

- O -

Offspring:
    only glorified beings can have spirit, 41,
    Brigham Young's teaching of producing spirit and body children, 42;
    Jesus Christ is literal, of Mary and God the Father, 58
Omnipotent:
    the Father and Son are, 145-147
Omnipresence:
    the Father and Son are, 147-150
Omniscience:
    the Father and Son are, 150-152
One:
    how the Father and Son are, 10;
    Lord tells Saints to be, 11
One God:
    Nephi's teaching of, 10,
    the three witnesses' teaching of, 10
Oneness of Deity:
    teaching of Charles W. Penrose of, 10;
Only Begotten Son:
    the Father's word of power is his, 12
Only true God, 14-15,
    Brigham Young's teaching of, 35-36
Other Women:
    saw the resurrected Lord, 114-115;
    Bruce R. McConkie's teaching who these, were, 115

- P -

Packer, Boyd K.:
    comments by, of those of the Twelve who have seen the resurrected Lord, 143-144
Paul, Apostle:
    11, 14-15, 22, 37-38, 116, 153, 156; saw the resurrected Lord, 121-122
Pearl of Great Price:
    writings of Moses in, 12-13;
    formation of man in writings of Abraham and Moses in the, 44
Penrose, Charles W.: 10
Personage of Spirit:
    Holy Ghost is a, 15
Peter:
    saw the resurrected Lord, 115-116;
    both Simon and Cephas are names of, 116
Petersen, Mark E.:
    saw the resurrected Lord, 142
Physical attributes:
    the Father, Son, and Holy Ghost, 15
Plan of Exaltation:
    personifies the eternal plan of salvation, 157
Plan of Salvation:
    the Father is the author of the, 14;

in conjunction with the plan
of exaltation, 157;
the gospel of Jesus Christ
is the, 156
Joseph F. Smith's teaching
of, 20;
George Q. Cannon's teaching
of, 20-21;
the gospel of Jesus Christ is
the, 23
Bruce R. McConkie's teaching
that the Father, not the Son, is
the Author of the, 87
Pratt, Orson:
6, 61-62, 146
Prayer:
true order of, 14;
Intercessory, 14
Priesthood:
Joseph Smith became an
apostle before receiving the, 7
Prophet Joseph Smith: See Smith,
Joseph

- R -

Redeemer:
God the second is the, 12, 16
Reformation:
reason for the, 4
Relationship of Mary and God:
Orson Pratt's teaching of, 61;
Brigham Young's teaching of,
62-63;
Joseph F. Smith's teaching
of, 63
Resurrected Lord:
Mary Magdalene and other
women saw the, 112-115;
Peter saw the, 115-116;
New Testament apostles and
disciples saw the, 117-118;
500 brethren; saw the, 118
Bruce R. McConkie's teaching
that the, appeared to unmentioned individuals, 120

James, the Lord's brother saw
the, 119-120
Revelation:
before fall all, came from
Jehovah, 13, 83;
after the fall all, comes from
Jesus Christ, 13, 83
Richards, George F.:
saw the resurrected Lord,
139-140
Rigdon, Sidney:
Joseph Smith and, saw the
Father and Son, 96, 126-127
Risen Lord: See Resurrected Lord
Roberts, B.H.: 16, 146, 148-149

- S -

Sacred Grove: See First Vision
Saul: See Paul
Savior: See Lord
Second:
Redeemer is God the, 12, 16
Seth:
saw the pre-mortal Lord, 101
Simon: See Peter
Smith, Hyrum:
teaching by, that he would
not serve a God that had not
all wisdom and power, 152
Smith, Joseph:
account of First Vision by, 4-7,
81-82; became witness of
Father and Son, 7-8;
when, became an apostle, 7;
teaching of everlasting
covenant of Godhead, 12;
teaching God once was a
mortal man, 18-19;
teaching of God is an exalted
man, 18-23;
teaching how we can become
exalted like God, 20;
teaching of a Father above
our Father, 21-22;
teaching of the Father laying

THE ETERNAL FATHER AND HIS SON

down his life, 22;
teaching that which is spiritual in likeness of that which is temporal, 43;
teaching of callings in Grand Council of heaven, 73;
the Father introduces his Son to, 81-84; ,
in the grove, saw the Father and Son, 95-96;
Sidney Rigdon and, saw the Father and Son, 96, 126-127;
at the Kirtland Temple, saw the Father and Son, 97, 127;
Zebedee Coltrin and , saw the Father and Son, 98-99, 128-129;
revealed the name of the Brother of Jared, 107;
Martin Harris and, saw the resurrected Lord, 125-126;
at the Kirtland Temple both Oliver Cowdery and , saw the resurrected Lord, 130

Smith, Joseph F., 19-20, 45, 63;
saw the resurrected Lord, 136-137;
teaching that God has all knowledge, 151

Smith, Joseph Fielding: 1-2, 7, 13, 17-18, 83, 149, 151-152,

Snow, Eliza R.: hymn of, 40-41

Snow, Lorenzo:
saw the resurrected Lord, 134-135

Solome:
the sister of Jesus' mother saw the resurrected Lord, 115

Solomon:
saw the premortal Lord, 106

Son:
Father and, appeared to Joseph Smith, 5-6, 11,
the Father appears and introduces his, 13;

Father and, have a body of flesh and bones, 15;
the , teaches his Father's gospel, 85-88;
the Son, not the Father, gives instructions, 87-88

Son of God:
Bruce R. McConkie's teaching that Adam and Christ are a, 47;
Jesus openly declared he was the, 89

Son of Man:
exalted name-title of Christ is, 25-26;
meaning of the name, 25-26;
the Son of God is the, who teaches the Father's gospel, 92

Sperry, Sidney B.: 79-80

Spirit:
Bruce R. McConkie's teaching of Jesus saying God is a, 90-91;
Joseph Smith Translation reads that Jesus said God promised his, 90-91

Stephen,
saw the Father and Son, 120

Supreme presidency:
Father, Son, and Holy Ghost comprise, 11

- T -

Talmage, James E: 2-3, 52, 56, 75-76, 85-87, 114, 120-122, 147

Testator:
God the third is the, 12, 16

Third:
Holy Ghost is God the, 12, 16

Times and Seasons:
Wentworth letter in, 9

Transfiguration:
the, of God's Son, 77; the, of Peter, James, and John, 78;

Trinity:
sectarian teachings of, 3;

teaching of Charles W.
Penrose on, 10
True God: only one, 14-15
True order of prayer: 14
Twelve years of age: See Boy-Jesus
Tyndale, William, 4

- U -

Unity:
 members of Godhead have perfect, 11;
 the Saints should have, 11

- V -

Virgin:
 Mary was a, 52-53; the, Mary was carried away in the Spirit, 53;
 Jesus Christ was born of a, birth, 54,

- W -

Wells, Rulon S.:
 saw the resurrected Lord, 138-139
Wentworth, John: 9;
Wentworth letter: 9
Wesley brothers, 4
Whitney, Orson F.:
 23, 37-38, 86, 147;
 saw the resurrected Lord, 140
Wight, Lyman,
 saw the Father and Son, 97-98, 124-125
Wilderness:
 Jesus was led by Spirit into the, 70
Williams, Frederick G.:
 saw the resurrected Lord, 129
Witness:
 God the third is the, 12, 16;
 Joseph Smith became only, for Christ, 7-8
Woman:
 man, Christ, the Father, and Adam was born of, 45-46
Woodruff, Wilford:
 saw the resurrected Lord, 133-134
Work and Glory: God's, 23
Worlds:
 without number, have been created, 12-13

- Y -

Young, Alfred Douglas:
 saw the Father and Son, 99, 131-132
Young, Brigham: 5, 19-20, 34-37, 42, 57, 62-63

ABOUT THE AUTHOR

Bruce E. Dana is an avid student of the gospel, a returned missionary with service in the Northwestern States and Pacific Northwest missions for the Church. He attended Weber State College and Utah State University. Brother Dana served several times as a Sunday School teacher, a Gospel Doctrine instructor, twice as a Sunday School president, and as a Stake Sunday School president. He served as a ward mission leader, and is currently a High Priest instructor in the Hyde Park, Utah Third Ward. Brother Dana is the father of eight children, and married to the former Brenda Lamb. He is employed as a coordinator by Schreiber Foods, Inc., in Logan, Utah.

Other books by Bruce E. Dana—*Glad Tidings Near Cumorah, The Three Nephites and Other Translated Beings, Mysteries of the Kingdom, Mary, Mother of Jesus,* and *Simon Peter.*

You can reach Bruce at: authorbrucedana@yahoo.com